BARRON'S
FOREIGN LANGUAGE GUIDES

Mastering
FRENCH
Grammar

P9-DEM-842

Michael Deneux

BARRON'S

Author: **Michael Deneux**
English translation: **Kathleen Luft**

All inquiries should be addressed to:
Barron's Educational Series, Inc.
250 Wireless Boulevard
Hauppauge, NY 11788
http://www.barronseduc.com

ISBN-10: 0-7641-3655-0
ISBN-13: 978-0-7641-3655-9
Library of Congress Control Number: 2006929369

Printed in China
9 8 7

How to Use This Book

Are you interested in improving your knowledge of French grammar? Maybe you want to review, practice, and add to what you already have learned—or even just look something up quickly? *Mastering French Grammar* will help you do all of that. This book presents and discusses all the essential features of French grammar using simple explanations, arranged in a way that is clear and easy to understand, and has plenty of helpful exercises.

How the Chapters Are Structured

First, in an introductory illustration accompanied by minidialogues, we present a selected aspect of French grammar in an everyday context.

Clear, easy-to-understand rules, neatly arranged tables, and detailed sections on usage provide a quick overview of the fundamentals. Ample numbers of practical, real-life examples show you the right way to use the grammatical element in question.

In the many exercises that follow, you have a chance to practice and apply what you have learned. Here the level of difficulty of an exercise is indicated by asterisks:
* = easy exercise; ** = moderately difficult exercise; *** = difficult exercise. This way you can easily monitor your own progress as you go.

In the marginal notes, you will find a great many helpful tips and information concerning correct usage:
▶ Introductory explanations of the grammatical phenomenon
▶ Tips to help you learn and additional hints
▶ Important exceptions and stumbling blocks
▶ References to other grammar chapters
▶ Vocabulary aids and help with translation

All the grammatical terms used in this book are listed in the overview on pages 229 and 230.

The index in the back of the book will help you find the right grammar information in a flash. To speed your search, important topics are given in red.

We wish you great success as you use this book as a reference tool and a means to improve and practice your French!

Table of Contents

Word Formation 9
Suffixes 9
Borrowings from Greek and Latin 12

The Noun 15
Gender 15
Formation of the Plural 17
Practice and Application 19

Noun Determiners 21
The Definite Article 21
The Indefinite Article 24
Practice and Application 26

Demonstrative Determiners 28
Practice and Application 30

Possessive Determiners 31
Practice and Application 34

Indefinite Determiners 35
Practice and Application 37

Interrogative Determiners 38
Practice and Application 40

Pronouns 41
Unstressed Personal Pronouns 41
Subject Pronouns 42
Direct Object Pronouns (Accusative Personal Pronouns) 42
Indirect Object Pronouns (Dative Personal Pronouns) 43
Reflexive Pronouns 44
Practice and Application 45

Adverbial Pronouns *y* and *en* 47
Placement of Object and Adverbial Pronouns 49
Practice and Application 51

Stressed (Disjunctive) Personal Pronouns 53
Practice and Application 54

Demonstrative Pronouns 55
Practice and Application 57

Contents

Possessive Pronouns   58
Practice and Application   59

Indefinite Pronouns: *tout, chacun, plusieurs, certains*   60
Practice and Application   62

Relative Pronouns   63
Practice and Application   66

The Verb   68
Tense   68
Mood   70

Present Tense   71
Overview of Verbs in the Present   73
Practice and Application   80

Compound Past and Past Participle   83
Past Participle   83
avoir or *être*?   84
Variability of the Past Participle   85
Practice and Application   88

Imperfect   92
Compound Past or Imperfect?   93
Practice and Application   95

Pluperfect   97
Practice and Application   98

Simple Past   100
Practice and Application   102

Simple Future   103
Near Future   106
Simple Future and Near Future   107
Practice and Application   108

Future Perfect   111
Practice and Application   112

Present Conditional   113
Past Conditional   115
Practice and Application   116

Present Subjunctive   118
Past Subjunctive   121
Obligatory Use of the Subjunctive   122
Optional Use of the Subjunctive   123
Present Subjunctive or Past Subjunctive   124
Practice and Application   125

Imperative   128
Replacement of the Imperative with Other Constructions   129
Practice and Application   130

Si Clause (Conditional Clause)   131
Practice and Application   133

Verbs with an Object   135
Reflexive Verbs   137
Impersonal Verbs and Expressions   139

Passive and Avoidance of the Passive   141
Practice and Application   143

Negation   144
oui, non, si   144
ne ... pas, ne ... plus, ne ... jamais, ne ... rien, ne ... personne,
ne ... aucun   144
Placement of Negations   144
Negation of Nouns   145
du tout   147
non plus   147
ne ... que and *seulement*   147
ne ... ni ... ni   147
Practice and Application   148

Indirect Discourse   151
Introduction of Subordinate Clauses   151
Change of Tense   152
Practice and Application   154

Adjectives   157
Masculine and Feminine Adjectives   157
Formation of the Plural   161
Special Features of the Agreement of Adjectives   162
Use   164
Placement Before or After the Noun   165
Comparison of Adjectives   168
Practice and Application   170

Contents

Adverbs   174
Formation of Adverbs Ending in *-ment*   175
Placement of Adverbs Ending in *-ment* That Are Not Derivatives   176
Comparatives of Adverbs   177
Adjectives Used as Adverbs   178
Adverbs Used as Adjectives   178
très, *beaucoup*, *bien*, and *tout*   179
Practice and Application   181

Numbers and Telling Time   183
Cardinal Numbers   183
Ordinal Numbers   185
Fractions   186
Collective Numbers   186
Telling Time   187
Giving the Date   188
Practice and Application   189

Prepositions   191
The Prepositions of Place *à*, *dans*, *en*   191
Other Prepositions of Place   193
Prepositions of Time   194
Modal Prepositions   196
Practice and Application   198

Conjunctions   201
Practice and Application   204

Declarative and Interrogative Sentences   206
The Declarative Sentence   206
The Interrogative Sentence   208
Practice and Application   213

Answers   215

Overview of Grammatical Terms   229

Index   231

Word Formation

In many cases, words consist of word stems and affixes (elements attached before or after a base or root). These elements are divided into two subcategories: prefixes and suffixes.

Suffixes

Suffixes can be used to form nouns, adjectives, and verbs. They are attached to a verb stem, an adjective, or a noun.

1. Suffixes for Formation of Nouns (Nominal Derivation)

Verb Stem + Suffix		
-ade	baigner	la baignade
	rigoler	la rigolade
-aison, -ison	cueillir	la cueillaison
	trahir	la trahison
-ance	allier	une alliance
	gérer	la gérance
-ateur, -atrice	ventiler	le ventilateur
	calculer	la calculatrice
-ement	loger	le logement
	agrandir	un agrandissement
-et, -ette	jouer	le jouet
	sonner	la sonnette
-eur, -euse	se balader	le baladeur
	coiffer	la coiffeuse
-oir, -oire	arroser	un arrosoir
	baigner	la baignoire
-tion	attribuer	une attribution
	finir	la finition
-ure	brûler	la brûlure
	piquer	la piqûre

Verb stem = verb without the infinitive ending -er / -ir / -re

la rigolade – *joke*

la calculatrice – *pocket calculator*

le baladeur – *pocket-sized music player*

Suffixes

Adjective + Suffix

-esse	fin, e	la finesse
	riche	la richesse
-ie	économe	une économie
	normand, e	la Normandie
-ise	bête	la bêtise
	franc, franche	la franchise
-té	beau, bel, belle	la beauté
	fier, fière	la fierté

la bêtise – *stupidity, foolishness*
la franchise – *frankness, sincerity*

Noun or Numeral + Suffix

-aine	dix	une dizaine
	cent	une centaine
-aire	la fonction	le fonctionnaire
	une action	un actionnaire
-eau, elle	un drap	un drapeau
	une rue	une ruelle
-et, -ette	un livre	un livret
	une maison	une maisonnette
-ie	un boulanger	la boulangerie
	le boucher	la boucherie
-ien, -ienne	l'Italie	un Italien
	Paris	une Parisienne
-ier, -ière	la pomme	le pommier
	la soupe	la soupière
-iste	la dent	le dentiste
	le journal	le journaliste
-on	une croûte	un croûton
	une veste	un veston

une dizaine – *around ten*
une centaine – *around one hundred*

le pommier – *apple tree*

2. Suffixes for Formation of Adjectives (Adjectival Derivation)

Verb Stem + Suffix

-able	habiter	habitable
	blâmer	blâmable
-eur, -euse	chercher	chercheur, -euse
	boiter	boiteux, -euse
-ible	lire	lisible
	corriger	corrigible

boiteux – *lame*

lisible – *readable, legible*

Substantiv + Suffix

-ien, -ienne	la Norvège	norvégien, -ienne
	l'Autriche	autrichien, -ienne
-in, -ine	l'enfant	enfantin, -e
	les Alpes	alpin, -e
-ais, -aise	le Franc	français, -e
	Lyon	lyonnais, -e
-ois, -oise	la Chine	chinois, -e
	le Luxembourg	luxembourgeois, -e
-ain, -aine	l'Amérique	américain, -e
	l'Afrique	africain, -e
-al, -ale	l'origine	original, -e
	la commune	communal, -e
-el, -elle	la fonction	fonctionnel, -elle
	la forme	formel, -elle
-if, -ive	l'instinct	instinctif, -ive
	le combat	combatif, -ive
-u, -ue	la bosse	bossu, -e
	le poil	poilu, -e

combatif – *combative, scrappy*

bossu – *humpbacked*

3. Suffixes Attached to Form Verbs (Verbal Derivation)

Noun + Suffix		
-er, -ter	le numéro la loge	numéroter loger
-iser	l'alcool le monopol	s'alcooliser monopoliser

Adjective + Suffix		
-er	bavard, -e gris, -e	bavarder se griser
-ifier	fort, -e simple	fortifier simplifier
-ir	maigre rouge	maigrir rougir
-iser	americain, -e légal, -e	americaniser légaliser

Borrowings from Greek and Latin

Many French affixes are borrowings from Latin and Greek.

If you are familiar with the prefixes or suffixes, you often can figure out the meaning of the word in question.

allonger – *to lengthen, extend*

1. Latin Prefixes

Prefix	Engl. Meaning	Example
a-, ad-	to, toward, near	allonger, adjoindre
ante-	before, in front of	antéposer, antécédent
dé-, dés-	opposite, away from	décharger, désavouer
dis-	apart, removed	une dissonance, la disgrâce
é-, ex-	out of	émigration, extraire

en-, em-	in	enterrer, emprisonner
in-, im-, il-, ir	not	un illettré, inconscient
inter-	between	l'intermédiaire, interdire
mal-	not	malhonnête, un malaise
mi-	half	à mi-temps, à mi-chemin
omni-	all	omniprésent, -e
plus-	more	plusieurs, le plus-que-parfait
pré-	in front of, before	un prénom, un prétexte
re-, ré-	again, back	reprendre, réagir
sou-, sous-	under, below	souligner, le sous-sol
sur-	over, above	le surlendemain, le survol

un illettré – *illiterate*

le surlendemain –
the day after tomorrow

2. Greek Prefixes

Prefix	Engl. Meaning	Example
a-, an-	opposite	anormal, -ale, amoral, -ale
aéro-	air	un aéroport, un aérodrome
dactylo-	finger	un dactylogramme
hélio-	sun	une héliothérapie
hippo-	horse	un hippodrome
laryngo-	larynx	une laryngite
odont-	tooth	une odontalgie
oto-	ears	un oto-rhino-laryngologiste
rhino-	nose	une rhinoscopie

un dactylogramme –
fingerprint

une odontalgie –
toothache

3. Latin Suffixes

Suffix	Engl. Meaning	Example
-cide	murderer, killer	un homicide, un insecticide
-cole	grow, cultivate	viticole, horticole
-culteur	grower, breeder	un apiculteur, un agriculteur
-fère	carry	pétrolifère, conifère
-vore	eater	carnivore

un homicide – *murderer*

carnivore –
meat-eating, carnivorous

4. Greek Suffixes

une gastralgie –
stomachache

un toxicomane –
drug addict

la kinésithérapie –
physical therapy

Suffix	Engl. Meaning	Example
-algie	pain	une gastralgie
-cratie	might, power	la démocratie
-graphe	writer, doer	un photographe, un télégraphe
-logie	science	la biologie, la psychologie,
-phie		la philosophie
-mane	addict	un toxicomane
-phile	fan, lover	un francophile
-phobe	enemy	un xénophobe
-thérapie	healing, therapy	la kinésithérapie

The Noun

1. la table
2. la chaise
3. l'assiette
4. le fromage
5. la souris
6. la fenêtre
7. le vase
8. les fleurs
9. le chat

1. the table – 2. the chair – 3. the plate – 4. the cheese – 5. the mouse –
6. the window – 7. the vase – 8. the flowers – 9. the cat

Gender

Voilà la voisine. Elle est médecin dans un hôpital.

There's the neighbor. She's a doctor in a hospital.

French has only two genders: masculine and feminine. There are no neuter nouns.

There are few fixed rules for recognizing the gender of a French noun. This is especially true for nouns that designate things.

> Therefore, you always need to learn the article along with the noun.

Basic Rules

A great many nouns have both a masculine form and a feminine form for designations of people and animals (animate nouns).

Gender

Nouns Referring to Persons

un Français – une Française
un Italien – une Italienne

un Allemand – une Allemande

un ouvrier – une ouvrière
un instituteur – une institutrice
un voisin – une voisine

un directeur – une directrice
un vendeur – une vendeuse

Nouns Referring to Animals

un chat – une chatte
un lion – une lionne

un chien – une chienne

For some designations of persons and animals, there are completely different words for the masculine and the feminine.

un parrain – *godfather*
une marraine –
godmother

un homme – une femme
un parrain – une marraine
un neveu – une nièce
un coq – une poule

un frère – une sœur
un garçon – une fille
un oncle – une tante

Some nouns have two genders, which are differentiated only by their articles.

un élève – une élève
un secrétaire – une secrétaire
un Belge – une Belge
un propriétaire – une propriétaire

un touriste – une touriste
un collègue – une collègue
un journaliste – une journaliste

For some nouns there is only a masculine form, which applies to both sexes.

In French, a woman who is a physician is also called "un médecin."

un écrivain
un auteur

un médecin
un pompier

Endings

The ending of some nouns indicates the grammatical gender.

Masculine Nouns

Nouns that end in **-isme**, **-oir**, **-teur**, **-ail**, **-al**, **-ier**, **-et**, **-ège** are always masculine.

le tourisme, le terrorisme
un moteur, un ordinateur
un canal, un hôpital
un billet, un guichet

un devoir, le pouvoir
un travail, un détail
un cahier, un métier
un collège, un manège

Nouns ending in **-age**, **-ment**, **-o/-ot**, **-on**, **-eau**, **-ent** usually are masculine, but here, too, there are exceptions!

un voyage, un garage
un vélo, un haricot
un bureau, un plateau

un département, un logement
un melon, un citron
le vent, le talent

> **Exceptions:** une image, une plage, une page, une jument, une photo, la météo, la peau, une dent

une jument – *mare*

Feminine Nouns

Nouns with the endings **-tié**, **-rie**, **-ance**, **-ence**, **-esse**, **-ette**, **-ise**, **-euse** are always feminine.

une amitié, une moitié
une correspondance, une alliance
la jeunesse, la finesse
une crise, une bise

une charcuterie, une boucherie
une différence, une influence
une bicyclette, une allumette
une friteuse, une perceuse

Nouns ending in **-ade**, **-ée**, **-ie**, **-ion**, **ité** are usually feminine. There are exceptions, however!

une promenade, une salade
une maladie, une librairie
une identité, une activité

une journée, une idée
une décision, une révision

> **Exceptions:** un stade, un lycée, un musée, un incendie, un million, un camion, un avion, un comité

Formation of the Plural

> J'ai acheté des pommes, un fromage et une bouteille de vin.

I bought some apples, a cheese, and a bottle of wine.

Basic Rule

Most nouns form the plural by adding **-s** to the singular.

un ami – des ami**s**
un homme – des homme**s**
un pain – des pain**s**

une chaise – des chaise**s**
une voiture – des voiture**s**
une pomme – des pomme**s**

Special Rules

Some nouns have an irregular plural. These include nouns ending in **-eu**, **-al**, **-eau**, **-ail**, and some nouns ending in **-ou**.

un f**eu** – des f**eux**
un mant**eau** – des mant**eaux**
un ch**ou** – des ch**oux**

un anim**al** – des anim**aux**
un trav**ail** – des trav**aux**

Formation of the Plural

Exceptions: Deviating from this rule, the following nouns form their plural by adding **-s**:

un bal – des bal**s**	un détail – des détail**s**
un pneu – des pneu**s**	un fou – des fou**s**
le cou – les cou**s**	le clou – les clou**s**

Nouns that end in **-s**, **-x**, and **-z** in the singular do not change in the plural.

un boi**s** – des boi**s**	un pri**x** – des pri**x**
un ne**z** – des ne**z**	

Some nouns have special forms in the plural.

monsieur – **mes**sieurs	**ma**dame – **mes**dames
mademoiselle – **mes**demoiselles	un **œil** – des **yeux**
un œuf – des œufs	With **des œufs**, **des bœufs**, and
un bœuf – des bœufs	**des os**, it's not the spelling, but
un os – des os	the pronunciation that must be carefully noted: **[dezø]**, **[debø]**, and **[dezo]**.

Some nouns exist only in the plural form or have a different meaning in the singular.

les ciseaux – *scissors*	**le** ciseau – *chisel*
les lunettes – *(eye)glasses*	**la** lunette – *telescope*
les toilettes – *toilet (WC)*	**la** toilette – *outfit, dress*

les environs, **les** épinards, **les** mathématiques

Proper names generally have no plural.

les Dutour, **les** Renault, **les** Hohenzollern

1. Form pairs: Fill in the missing masculine or feminine nouns. *

a) un danseur   <u>une danseuse</u>

b) un neveu   _____

c) _____   une reine

d) un instituteur   _____

e) _____   une camarade

f) _____   une criminelle

g) un peintre   _____

h) _____   une duchesse

i) un invité   _____

j) _____   une victime

2. Translate the following nouns into English. *

a) le livre   <u>the book</u>   la livre   <u>the pound</u>

b) le critique _____   la critique _____

c) le parti _____   la partie _____

d) le poêle _____   la poêle _____

e) le tour _____   la tour _____

f) le moral _____   la morale _____

3. Fill in the blanks with the plural form of each singular noun below. **

a) le cheval   <u>les chevaux</u>   g) le cou   _____

b) le détail _____   h) le canal   _____

c) le mal _____   i) le bateau   _____

d) le bijou _____   j) le gaz   _____

e) le cours _____   k) l'os   _____

f) l'œil _____

4. Divide the following terms into masculine and feminine nouns. Write them, along with their definite articles, in the table below, and form the plural. **

monsieur, Espagnole, chienne, adolescente, ouvrier, actrice, Belge, secrétaire, médecin, romantisme, mouchoir, ordinateur, fusée, baguette, détail, cheval, prix, maladie, décision, nez, œil, bal, perceuse, révision, différence, soleil, crise, bois, faiblesse, hôtel, image, dent.

Masculine Nouns

Singular	Plural	Feminine Nouns Singular	Plural
le monsieur	les messieurs		

Noun Determiners

1. So you really want to buy cheese and a bottle of red wine here?
2. I like this delicatessen a lot. 3. All these products are too expensive.

Determiners are words that occur only in connection with nouns. They must be distinguished from pronouns, which take the place of a noun.

▶ **Pronouns,** p. 41

The Definite Article

Forms

	Masculine	Feminine
Singular	**le** monsieur **l'**hôtel	**la** dame **l'**histoire
Plural	**les** messieurs **les** hôtels	**les** dames **les** histoires

Nouns that begin with vowels or a "silent h" normally use **l'**, rather than le or la, as the definite article.

l'animal	**l'enfant**	**l'**idée
l'or	**l'u**sine	**l'**hôtel

The Definite Article

Some nouns beginning with h do not use l', but **le** or **la**, as the definite article.

> In dictionaries, such an h is preceded by a little mark: 'h.

le haricot   **le** Hollandais   **la** halte
le handicap   **le** hareng   **le** hold-up
le héros

Contraction of the Definite Article

Ce soir, le président sera à la télévision.
①

Je pense aux prochaines vacances.
②

C'est le bureau du patron.
③

1. This evening the president will be on television. 2. I'm thinking about the next vacation.
3. That's the office of the boss.

à + l̶e̶   ▶ au
à + l̶e̶s̶ ▶ aux

The definite article **le** always contracts with the preposition **à** to form **au**, and the article **les** always contracts with this preposition to form **aux**. **A** and **la**, however, do not contract.

Michel va **au** café.
Il va **aux** Pays-Bas.

Il va **à la** piscine.

d̶e̶ + l̶e̶   ▶ du
d̶e̶ + l̶e̶s̶ ▶ des

The definite articles **le** and **les** always contract with the preposition **de** to to form **du** and **des**, respectively. **De** and **la** do not contract.

Michel revient **du** café.
Il revient **des** Pays-Bas.

Il vient **de la** piscine.

Use

The definite article is used in French to refer to specific nouns and to indicate the general sense of a noun.

Demain, nous irons chez **les** Dutour.
Le chancelier Schröder a fait un voyage officiel en France.
Ma fille a consulté **le** docteur Petit.
Bonsoir, Madame **le** Professeur.

> But: Bonjour, docteur.
> Bonjour, professeur.

!

The definite article is used:
- before surnames and before titles, if the surname follows.
- in addressing someone, if the title follows.

J'aime **la** France, **la** Suisse, **le** Portugal, **l'**Australie,
l'Alsace, **la** Corse et **les** Landes.

- before geographical names (countries, continents, provinces, *départements*, and larger islands).

Le matin, je dors jusqu'à sept heures.
Mais demain matin, je peux dormir jusqu'à neuf heures.

Le lundi, les musées sont fermés.
Mais lundi prochain, ils seront ouverts.

- with times of day and days of the week, only to indicate habitual recurrence ("every morning," "on Mondays").

Aujourd'hui, nous sommes mardi.
Aujourd'hui, nous sommes **le** jeudi 10 mai.

- with a day of the week when followed by the date.

Il **aime les** fruits et il **déteste les** légumes.
Et moi, j'**adore le** lait.
Mais je n'aime **pas les** pommes.

- after **aimer**, **détester**, **adorer**, and similar verbs expressing emotion, in negated sentences as well.

L'argent n'a pas d'odeur.
Les citrons sont riches en vitamine C.

> The article is not used in this sense in English.

- to express general truths or concepts.

The Indefinite Article

1. Go buy some oranges and some flour. 2. How much do we need?
3. Buy a kilo of oranges and a package of flour.

Forms

	Countable Nouns Masculine	Feminine	Uncountable Nouns Masculine	Feminine
Singular	**un** monsieur	**une** dame	du lait	de la tarte
	un hôtel	**une** histoire	de l'ail	de l'eau
Plural	**des** messieurs	**des** dames	–	–
	des hôtels	**des** histoires	–	–

The indefinite article is used in French before nouns referring to nonspecific items or to unknown specific items.
Caution: Unlike the English indefinite article, the French indefinite article has a plural.

In English, the French plural indefinite article may be translated as *some* or may be omitted.

He is buying (some) oranges. – *Il achète* ***des*** *oranges.*

Use

J'ai **un** bon copain.
On va regarder **des** photos et écouter **des** CD.

Un, **une**, and **des** are used before nonspecific persons or countable things in the singular or plural.

On va boire **de l'**eau minérale et on va manger **du** pain avec **du** fromage.
Comme dessert il y aura **de la** tarte au citron.

Du, **de la**, and **de l'** are used to refer to an unspecified quantity of uncountable things.

Tu bois **un verre d'**eau ?
Tu prends **une tranche de** pain et **un peu de** fromage ?
Tu veux **un morceau de** tarte ? – Oui, je veux **beaucoup de** tarte !

▮ After most quantities, use only **de** + noun, without an article.

Tu prends encore un verre d'eau ? – Non, je ne veux **plus d'**eau.
Tu veux une pomme ? – Non, **pas de** pomme.

▮ When negating nouns, as when stating quantities, use only **pas de**
or **plus de**.

▶ On negation, see
the section beginning
on p. 144

La plupart des gens ont dormi.
Une partie des gens ont chanté.
Il reste encore **la moitié de la** tarte et **la plus grande partie des**
fruits.

▮ In the expressions of quantity above, **de** is always followed by the
complete article.

Fixed Expressions

In certain fixed expressions, no article is used.

Il a soif / faim / peur.	*He is thirsty / hungry / afraid.*
Il a besoin d'une voiture.	*He needs a car.*
Il a raison / tort.	*He is right / wrong.*

In some phrases, however, the definite article is used where English would
require no article.

Il regarde **la** télé.	*He is watching television.*
Il écoute **la** musique.	*He is listening to music.*
Il apprend **l'**anglais.	*He is learning English.*

Practice and Application

Articles

1. Fill in the blanks with **un**, **une**, or **des**. *

a) _une_ chemise

b) _____ cravate

c) _____ pantalon

d) _____ chaussures

e) _____ tailleur

f) _____ slips

g) _____ T-shirts

h) _____ blouson

i) _____ veste

j) _____ gilet

k) _____ chaussettes

l) _____ pull

2. Everyone in the Dupont family is looking for something. Fill in the missing definite articles and **est** or **sont**. *

a) Où __est__ __la__ voiture de ma femme ?

b) Où _____ _____ jouets de nos enfants ?

c) Où _____ _____ clé de _____ voiture ?

d) Où _____ _____ assiettes de _____ grand-mère ?

e) Où _____ _____ verres de _____ vitrine ?

f) Où _____ _____ ordinateur de _____ voisine ?

g) Où _____ _____ CD de _____ Michel ?

3. What ingredients do you need to make crèpes? Fill in **le, la, les, un, une, du, de la, de, des** or nothing at all. **

a) Il faut mettre d'abord 500 grammes _de_ farine.

b) Faites _____ trou au centre et versez _____ trois œufs.

c) Puis ajoutez 20 grammes _____ beurre et trois grammes _____ sel.

d) Versez _____ centilitre _____ bière et _____ quart _____ litre de lait.

e) Mélangez _____ pâte.

f) Puis versez 125 grammes _____ beurre fondu.

g) Laissez reposer la pâte environ 45 _____ minutes.

h) Ajoutez _____ lait si _____ pâte est trop épaisse.

i) Mettez _____ mince couche _____ pâte dans _____ poêle graissée.

j) Faites cuire _____ crêpe d'un côté puis retournez-là.

k) Mettes sur _____ crêpe _____ jambon, _____ fromage, _____ œuf ou

_____ légumes.

l) On accompagne _____ crêpes bretonnes avec _____ bolée _____ cidre.

m) Je vous souhaite _____ bon appétit.

4. Decide what is needed: **le**, **la**, **les**, **un**, **une**, **des**, **du**, **de l'**, **de la**, **de**, or nothing at all. **

a) • Bonjour, madame, je voudrais __du__ lait.

   ○ Combien _____ lait voulez-vous ?

   • Je voudrais trois bouteilles _____ lait.

b) • Et il me faut _____ fromage. Je prends trois tranches _____

   gruyère et _____ peu _____ fromage râpé.

   ○ Je n'ai pas _____ fromage râpé aujourd'hui.

   • Ça ne fait rien, je prends _____ camembert.

> Use of the article in negations, p. 145

c) • Qu'est-ce que vous avez comme _____ fruits aujourd'hui?

   ○ J'ai _____ pommes, _____ oranges, _____ kiwis et _____ ananas.

   • Ah, j'aime _____ kiwis. Mais je n'aime pas _____ ananas.

   Elles coûtent combien _____ oranges ?

   ○ Deux euros trente.

   • Alors, donnez-moi _____ kilo _____ pommes et six ___ kiwis.

d) • Vous avez _____ fraises ?

   ○ Non, je n'ai pas _____ fraises. _____ plupart _____ gens

   n'achètent pas chez moi. Ils préfèrent _____ supermarché.

   Là, _____ plus grande partie _____ fruits est moins chère.

e) • Ça sera tout, madame. Vous me faites _____ addition !

   ○ Ça vous fera 18 euros quinze.

   • Voilà _____ billet _____ 20 euros.

   ○ Et voilà _____ monnaie.

   • Au revoir.

   ○ Au revoir et à _____ prochaine.

Demonstrative Determiners

1. Do you like this shirt? 2. No, I prefer that sweater.
3. And what do you think of this parka? 4. No. But I really like these jeans.

Ce, cet, cette, ces

Forms

	Singular Noun	Plural Noun
Masculine	**ce** monsieur / **cet** hôtel	**ces** messieurs / **ces** hôtels
Feminine	**cette** dame / **cette** histoire	**ces** dames / **ces** histoires

The demonstrative determiner **ces** (= *these, those*) should not be confused with the possessive determiner **ses** (= *his, her, its;* see p. 31).

Use

Tu as vu **cette** fille ?
Tu peux m'expliquer **cette** phrase ?
On va au cinéma **ce** soir ?

Demonstrative determiners placed before nouns indicate that persons or things are near the speaker in terms of space or time.

| **ce** matin | *this morning* | **cet** après-midi | *this afternoon* |
| **ce** soir | *this evening* | **cette** nuit | *tonight* |

The demonstrative determiner is used in connection with times of day.

The demonstrative determiner **cet** is used only with masculine nouns that begin with a vowel or a "silent h."

> **cet** hôtel, **cet** anorak, **cet** homme

Caution: With some masculine nouns beginning with **h**, **ce** is retained.

> **ce** haricot, **ce** Hollandais, **ce** handicap

With feminine nouns, **cette** is always used.

> **cette** église, **cette** histoire, **cette** idée, **cette** femme

In dictionaries, such an h is preceded by a little mark: ´h.

▶ See **Definite Article**, p. 21

Ce...-là, cet...-là, cette...-là

Especially in the spoken language, **-là** may be appended to the noun modified by **ce** / **cet** / **cette** / **ces**, to emphasize what is being referred to.

> Tu connais **cet** homme-**là** ?
> **Cette** robe-**là** me plaît.

If two different things are referred to in a sentence, the noun is linked to the particles **-ci** or **-là**. In this case, **-ci** refers to the first-mentioned or closer noun, and **-là** to the noun mentioned second or located farther away.

> Tu préfères **cette** photo-**ci** ou **cette** photo-**là** ?
> Voulez-vous **ce** sandwich-**ci** ou **ce** sandwich-**là** ?

Demonstrative Determiners

1. Olivier wants a new outfit. His girlfriend asks him: "Qu'est-ce que tu penses de … " Add the appropriate demonstrative determiners. *

« Qu'est-ce que tu penses de … »

a) _ce__ blouson ?   b) _____ pantalon ?

c) _____ chemise ?   d) _____ slip ?

e) _____ chaussettes ?   f) _____ T-shirt ?

g)_____ pull-over ?   h) _____ cravate ?

i) _____ ceinture ?   j) _____ veste ?

k) _____ chaussures ?   l) _____ sweat ?

Possessive Determiners

1. Il cherche sa clé.

2. Elle cherche sa clé.

3. Ils cherchent leur clé.

4. Ils cherchent leurs clés.

---

1. He is looking for his key. 2. She is looking for her key. 3. They are looking for their key.
4. They are looking for their keys.

1. Only One Owner

Forms

	Singular Noun		Plural Noun
	Masculine Noun	Feminine Noun	Masculine or Feminine Noun
Je cherche	**mon** père **mon** ami	**ma** mère **mon** amie	**mes** parents **mes** amis / **mes** amies
Tu cherches	**ton** père **ton** ami	**ta** mère **ton** amie	**tes** parents **tes** amis / **tes** amies
Il cherche	**son** père **son** ami	**sa** mère **son** amie	**ses** parents **ses** amis / **ses** amies
Elle cherche	**son** père **son** ami	**sa** mère **son** amie	**ses** parents **ses** amis / **ses** amies

2. Several Owners

Forms

	Singular Noun (masculine or feminine)	Plural Noun (masculine or feminine)
Nous cherchons	**notre** père / **notre** mère **notre** ami / **notre** amie	**nos** parents **nos** amis / **nos** amies
Vous cherchez	**votre** père / **votre** mère **votre** ami / **votre** amie	**vos** parents **vos** amis / **vos** amies
Ils cherchent	**leur** père / **leur** mère **leur** ami / **leur** amie	**leurs** parents **leurs** amis / **leurs** amies

A possessive determiner that refers to a singular noun never ends in **-s**.

> J'ai vu **mon** frère.
> Ils ne trouvent pas **leur** voiture.
> Il me montre **sa** nouvelle bicyclette.
> Elle attend **son** amie.

A possessive determiner that refers to a plural noun always ends in **-s**.

> Je ne trouve plus **mes** photos.
> Il joue avec **ses** enfants.
> Ils lisent **leurs** livres.
> Nous sortons avec **nos** copines.

In the singular, you must distinguish between masculine and feminine nouns in choosing a possessive determiner. Masculine nouns are always preceded by **mon**, **ton**, **son**, and feminine ones by **ma**, **ta**, **sa**.

> Elle parle avec **son** copain.   *She is speaking with **her** boyfriend.*
> Il sort avec **sa** copine.   *He is going out with **his** girlfriend.*

With feminine nouns or adjectives beginning with a vowel or a "silent h," also use **mon**, **ton**, **son**.

> Il embrasse **son** amie.
> Elle a vu **son** ancienne voisine.

! But: **sa huppe**

huppe – *crest, tuft*

Where the third person is concerned, you always need to know whether there is only one owner (then: **son**, **sa**, **ses**) or more than one (then: **leur**, **leurs**).

Il attend **sa** copine.
Elle attend **sa** copine.
} only one owner

Ils attendent **leur** copain.
Ils attendent **leurs** copains.
} two or more owners

Unlike English, French does not differentiate between "<u>his</u> mother" and "<u>her</u> mother." The choice of the possessive determiners depends solely on the following noun, the "possession."

Il va voir **sa** mère.   Il va voir **son** père.
Elle va voir **sa** mère.   Elle va voir **son** père.

Votre and **vos** also serve as polite forms for people whom you address with the polite pronoun **vous**.

Voilà **votre** thé, madame.
Votre attention, s'il vous plaît.
Je ne trouve pas **vos** lettres, monsieur.

Do not confuse the possessive determiners **leur** and **leurs** with the pronoun **leur**, which takes the place of the object of the preposition **à**.

▶ See p. 43

Est-ce que tu téléphones à tes parents ?
– Oui , je **leur** téléphone tout de suite. *(... I'll call **them** ...)*

Practice and Application

1. **Son**, **sa**, **ses**, **leur**, or **leurs**? Fill in each blank with the correct possessive determiner. ***

a) Yves est le frère d'Olivier.

Il est __son__ frère.

b) Olivier est le frère de Barbara.

Il est _____ frère.

c) Michèle est la mère d'Olivier.

Elle est _____ mère.

d) Pascal est le père de Barbara.

Il est _____ père.

e) Yves, Olivier et Barbara sont les enfants de Michèle.

Ils sont _____ enfants.

f) Olivier est le fils de Michèle et Pascal.

Il est _____ fils.

g) Barbara est la fille de Michèle et Pascal.

Elle est _____ fille.

h) Yves, Olivier et Barbara sont les enfants de Michèle et Pascal.

Ils sont _____ enfants.

Indefinite Determiners: *tout, chaque, plusieurs, certain*

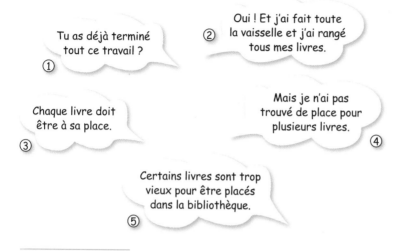

① Tu as déjà terminé tout ce travail ?

② Oui ! Et j'ai fait toute la vaisselle et j'ai rangé tous mes livres.

③ Chaque livre doit être à sa place.

④ Mais je n'ai pas trouvé de place pour plusieurs livres.

⑤ Certains livres sont trop vieux pour être placés dans la bibliothèque.

1. Have you already finished all the work? 2. Yes! And I did all the dishes and put away all my books. 3. Each book has to be in the right place. 4. But I didn't find any room for several books. 5. Certain books are too old to be put in the bookcase.

Tout, toute, tous, toutes

Forms

	Singular Noun	Plural Noun
Masculine	**tout l'**appartement	**tous les** appartements
Feminine	**toute la** maison	**toutes les** maisons

> **Tout** never stands alone before a noun!

Tout... agrees in number and gender with the following noun. Between **tout** ... and the noun, there must always be an additional determiner: the definite article, the possessive determiner, or the demonstrative determiner.

tous les livres
tous mes livres
tous ces livres

▶ For **tous** as a pronoun, see p. 60

Before expressions of time and in colloquial speech, **tout** ... is also followed by the indefinite article.

toute une nuit
toute une histoire

In English, the singular **tout** and **toute** + determiner is translated as "all, every, entire, (the) whole (of)," whereas the plural **tous** and **toutes** + determiner is rendered as "all, every."

toute la maison	*the whole house*
tous les livres	*all the books*

Chaque

Chaque (each, every) is invariable in number and gender and precedes only singular nouns. It takes the place of an article.

chaque livre
chaque maison

Whereas **tout / toutes les** always means "all" without distinction, **chaque** is used to emphasize each one individually.

Tous les hommes sont égaux mais **chaque** homme est différent.

Plusieurs

Plusieurs (many, several) is invariable in number and gender and takes the place of an article before plural nouns.

Je t'ai téléphoné **plusieurs** fois.
Plusieurs personnes se sont réunies dans la rue.

Certain, certaine, certains, certaines

Forms

	Singular Noun	Plural Noun
Masculine	**un certain** M. Dutour	**certains** adultes
Feminine	**une certaine** Mme Dutour	**certaines** personnes

Certain... (certain) is variable and agrees in number and gender with the noun it modifies. As in English, the indefinite article is used before **certain / certaine** only in the singular.

Il restera **un certain** temps.
Une certaine Mme Dutour est à la porte.
Dans **certains pays** les enfants travaillent toute la journée.
Certaines personnes ne disent pas la vérité.

1. Fanny and Emma like to eat a lot.

Answer these questions with **tout le / toute la / tous les** or **toutes les**. *

a) Il y a encore des pommes ?

   – Non, elles ont mangé   <u>toutes les pommes.</u>

b) Il reste encore des kiwis ?

   – Non, elles ont mangé   <u> </u>.

c) Et l'ananas ?

   – Non, <u> </u>

d) Elles ont laissé des spaghetti ?

   – Non, <u> </u>

e) Il y avait une bouteille de limonade.

   – Mais <u> </u>

f) Il y avait aussi cinq bananes.

   – Oui, mais <u> </u>

2. Using **certain**, create sentences, and pay close attention to the use of the article. **

a) personnes – penser – être la faute des étrangers

   <u>Certaines personnes pensent que c'est la faute des étrangers</u>.

b) Monsieur Gilles – dire – la musique être très importante

   <u> </u>.

c) enfants – ne pas dire la vérité

   <u> </u>.

d) nombre de personnes – avoir disparu

   <u> </u>.

e) Il restera – temps

   <u> </u>.

f) pays – les gens – ne pas avoir assez à manger

   <u> </u>.

Interrogative Determiners

1. What a soccer match last night! 2. Who are your favorite players?
3. And which teams do you like?

Forms

	Singular Noun	Plural Noun
Masculine	**quel** avion	**quels** avions
Feminine	**quelle** ville	**quelles** villes

Quel... always directly precedes the noun and agrees with it in number and gender.

> **Quel** chauffeur conduira le car ?
> **Quels** pays est-ce que vous connaissez ?

Quel... also can be linked with être. Then it agrees with the following noun in number and gender.

> **Quelle** est votre ville préférée ?
> **Quels** sont les livres de Pascale ?

Use

Tu as **quel** âge ?
Vous avez **quelle** heure ?
On est **quel** jour aujourd'hui ?
Vous avez visité **quelles** villes ?

Colloquial speech

Especially in colloquial French, **quel** ... is not placed first in the sentence but follows the verb.

Quel âge avez-vous ?
Quelle voiture préferez-vous ?

Quel... is used as an interrogative determiner of the noun in questions that refer to a noun.

Quelle jolie maison !
Quelles idées !
Quel menteur !

As an expression of amazement, **quel / quelle** usually is translated as "what a."

Quel... can also be used to express amazement or surprise.

Special Phrases with *quel...*

Quel âge avez-vous ?	*How old are you?*
Quelle heure est-il ?	*What time is it?*
Quel jour sommes-nous aujourd'hui ?	*What day is today?*
Quelle est votre taille ?	*What is your size?*
Quelle est votre adresse ?	*What is your address?*

Interrogative Determiners

1. You are interviewing Madame Le Grand. Ask her questions using quel / quelle / quels / quelles! *

a) ___Quel___ âge avez-vous ?

b) _____ est votre adresse ?

c) _____ sont vos actrices préférées ?

d) _____ pays est-ce que vous connaissez ?

e) _____ est votre ville préférée ?

f) A Paris, dans _____ restaurant est-ce que vous allez manger ?

g) Votre mari, _____ sports pratique-t-il ?

h) _____ sont vos projets pour l'été prochain ?

Pronouns

Pronouns are words that take the place of a noun. They must be differentiated from the noun determiners. French has unstressed (**je**, **tu...**, **le**, **la...**, **lui**, **leur...**) and stressed, or disjunctive, personal pronouns (**moi**, **toi...**).

▶ On the **determiners**, see the section starting on p. 21

Unstressed Personal Pronouns

Unstressed personal pronouns are used only in conjunction with a verb.

① Est-ce que tu as vu ta sœur ?

② Non, je ne l'ai pas vue.

③ Est-ce que tu vas téléphoner à ta sœur ?

④ Non, je ne vais pas lui téléphoner.

⑤ Mais je vais la voir demain.

1. Have you seen your sister? 2. No, I haven't seen her. 3. Are you going to telephone your sister? 4. No, I'm not going to telephone her. 5. But I'm going to see her tomorrow.

Subject Pronoun	Direct Object Pronoun	Indirect Object Pronoun
Je n'aime plus Yves. **Je** vais lui parler.	Pourquoi est-ce que tu ne **m'**aimes plus ?	Pourquoi est-ce que tu veux **me** parler ?
Tu exagères.	Je **t'**invite au restaurant.	Je **te** raconterai toute l'histoire.
Voilà Yves. **Il** a faim. Voilà Yvette. **Elle** a faim aussi.	Il **la** trouve sympa. Elle **le** trouve sympa aussi.	Il **lui** dit bonjour. Elle **lui** fait une bise.
Nous irons au Cygne ?	D'accord ! J'aimerais que les voisins **nous** accompagnent.	Ils pourront **nous** montrer les photos du voyage.
Vous irez au Cygne ?	On va **vous** accompagner.	On va **vous** montrer les photos.
Voilà les voisins. **Ils** ont faim aussi.	Ils **les** accompagnent.	Ils **leur** montrent les photos.

Subject pronoun = nominative pronoun; direct object pronoun = accusative pronoun; indirect object pronoun = dative pronoun

Subject Pronouns

J'ai une sœur. Elle habite à Paris.

I have a sister. She lives in Paris.

Subject pronouns take the place of a noun that is the subject of a sentence.

Yves a faim. ▶ **Il** a faim.   **Yvette** a faim. ▶ **Elle** a faim.

Forms

je/j'	before a vowel or a "silent h," **je** becomes **j'** ▶ Je dors. J'aide mon frère.
on	is translated as "one," or, in colloquial speech, as "we," "you," "they," or "someone."
vous	means "you" (plural of the familiar **tu**, or polite form)
ils	takes the place of a plural masculine noun (**les cafés**) or of several nouns that are either all masculine (**Yves et Michel**) or a mixture of masculine and feminine (**Yves et Yvette**)
elles	takes the place of a plural feminine noun (**les voitures**) or of several feminine nouns (**Yvette et Paulette**)

Direct Object Pronouns (Accusative Personal Pronouns)

In English, direct object pronouns usually answer the questions "whom?" or "what?"

Il m'a rendu visite hier soir.

He visited me yesterday evening.

The direct object pronouns take the place of a noun that is a direct object. Direct objects can be identified by the absence of a preposition before the noun in question.

Elle n'aime plus **Yves**.   ▶ Elle ne **l'**aime plus.
Ils accompagnent **Yves et Yvette**. ▶ Ils **les** accompagnent.

Forms

me / m'	Il **me** regarde. Il **m'**invite au restaurant.
te / t'	Il **te** regarde. Il **t'**invite au restaurant.
le / l'	Elle **le** regarde. Elle **l'**invite.
	▶ **le** takes the place of a masculine noun.
la / l'	Il **la** regarde. Il **l'**invite.
	▶ **la** takes the place of a feminine noun.
nous	Ils **nous** regardent ? Ils **nous** accompagnent ?
vous	Oui, on **vous** regarde. On **vous** accompagne.
les	Ils **les** trouvent sympa.
	▶ **les** takes the place of a plural noun.

! Before a vowel and a "silent h," **me, te, le, la** become **m', t', l', l'**.

▶ On the placement of the object pronouns, see p. 49

Indirect Object Pronouns (Dative Personal Pronouns)

> Il m'a écrit une lettre.

▶ On the effect that preceding direct object pronouns have on the past participle, see p. 86

He has written me a letter.

The indirect object pronouns take the place of a noun that is an indirect (dative) object. Indirect objects can be identified by the presence of the preposition **à** before the noun in question. In English, indirect objects generally answer the question "to whom?" or "for whom?"

Elle n'écrit plus **à Yves**. ▶ Elle ne **lui** écrit plus.
Il dit bonjour **à Yvette**. ▶ Il **lui** dit bonjour.

Forms

me / m'	Tu **me** racontes l'histoire ? Tu **m'**offres un café ?
te / t'	Oui, je **te** raconte l'histoire. Et je **t'**offre un café.
lui	Il **lui** raconte toute l'histoire. Elle **lui** donne un bisou.
	▶ **lui** takes the place of a masculine or feminine singular noun.
nous	Est-ce que les voisins vont **nous** montrer les photos ?
vous	Oui, on va **vous** montrer les photos.
leur	Ils **leur** montrent les photos. Ils **leur** offrent l'apéritif.
	▶ **leur** takes the place of a masculine or feminine plural noun.

! Before a "silent h," **me** and **te** become **m'** and **t'**.

▶ Possessive deter-
miners: see p. 32

Caution: Don't confuse the indirect object pronoun **leur** with the possessive determiners **leur** and **leurs**!

▶ Unstressed personal
pronouns: see p. 53

The indirect object pronoun **lui** represents both masculine and feminine nouns. It must not be confused with the stressed (disjunctive) personal pronoun **lui**, which substitutes only for masculine nouns.

    Elle **lui** offre un café.   ▶ indirect object pronoun, (*to*) *him / her*
    Elle parle de **lui**.   ▶ stressed object pronoun, *about him*

Reflexive Pronouns

Mon ami s'appelle Pierre.

My friend is named Pierre.

Reflexive verbs are verbs whose infinitive includes the reflexive pronoun.

Reflexive pronouns are required with reflexive verbs. Such verbs need a reflexive pronoun in addition to the subject pronoun because the subject is performing the action on itself. In the first and second persons, the reflexive pronouns are identical to the object pronouns. Only in the third person do they have a different form.

▶ For more on reflex-
ive verbs, see p. 137

me / m'	Je **me** marierai avec Yvette. Je **m'**excuserai de ma conduite.
te / t'	Tu ne **te** défends pas contre l'accusation ?
se / s'	Il **se** défend. Il **s'**adresse à Yvette.
nous	Nous **nous** marierons dans un mois.
vous	Vous **vous** connaissez depuis longtemps ?
se / s'	Ils **se** connaissent depuis un an seulement.

1. Help with the search!

Answer the questions by using **le**, **la**, **les**. Pay attention to the agreement of the participle! **

a) Est-ce que tu as vu mes clés ?

Non, _je ne les ai pas vues_____ .

b) Est-ce que tu as vu mon porte-monnaie ?

_____

c) Tu sais où sont mes cigarettes ?

Non, _____ vues.

d) Mais où sont mes lunettes ?

Je _____ .

e) Je ne trouve plus mon livre de français. Tu l'as vu ?

Non, _____ .

f) Et mon dictionnaire ? Où est-ce qu'il est ?

Je ne sais pas. Je _____ .

g) Mon Dieu ! Où est ma bouteille de cognac ?

Je ne sais pas. Je _____ .

2. Replace the words in bold with the appropriate personal pronouns. **

a) Yvette dit **à Paulette** : « Moi et Yves, nous avons des problèmes.

_Yvette lui dit :_____

b) Je n'aime plus **Yves**.

_____

c) **Yves** admire trop **Claudine**.

_____

d) Il trouve **Claudine** sympa.

_____

e) Il téléphone **à Claudine** tous les jours.

_____

f) Et **Claudine** a demandé **à Yves les clés de la maison**.

   _____

g) Et **Yves** attend **Claudine** à la maison.

   _____

h) Mais **la maison** appartient **à moi et à ma sœur**.

   _____

i) Nous avons acheté **cette maison**.

   _____

j) De toute façon, je n'accepte plus **cette situation**.

   _____

k) Je vais quitter **Yves**.

   _____

l) Et je vais jeter dehors **Yves et Claudine**.

   _____

m) La semaine prochaine, je vais raconter **toute l'histoire à ma sœur**.

   _____

n) **Yves** n'a jamais compris **ma situation personnelle**. »

   _____

Adverbial Pronouns *y* and *en*

1. *Do you take milk in your coffee? 2. No, thank you, I don't.*
3. *Are you interested in sports? 4. Yes, I'm very interested in them.*

Use

Est-ce que tu veux répondre **à la lettre de tes parents** ?
– Oui, j'**y** réponds tout de suite.

y substitutes for indirect objects (dative objects) that are linked to the verb by **à** and refer to things …

Est-ce que tu vas **à Paris** ? – Oui, j'**y** vais.
Tu vas **chez le dentiste** ? – Non, je n'**y** vais pas.

… and stands for locations that are introduced by **à**, **en**, **dans**, **chez**, **sur**, **sous**, etc.

Est-ce qu'il parle **de son travail** ? – Non, il n'**en** parle jamais.

en substitutes for indirect objects (dative objects) that are linked to the verb by **de** and refer to things …

Est-ce que tu viens **de Paris** ? – Oui, j'**en** viens.

… locations that are introduced by **de** …

Adverbial Pronouns y *and* en

Je voudrais **des pommes**. – Combien **en** voulez-vous ?
J'**en** voudrais **un kilo**. – Et **du lait**.
Combien **de bouteilles** ? – Donnez-m'**en** deux.

▌ ... as well as complements that are introduced by the indefinite
article. In this case, a quantity (**un kilo**) or a number (**deux**)
usually is added.

Generally, persons are not replaced with **y** or **en**. Instead, use:

Est-ce que tu réponds **à ta mère** ? – Non, je ne **lui** réponds jamais.

▌ - an indirect object pronoun with objects that include **à**.

Est-ce que tu penses souvent **à ton amie** ?
– Oui, je pense souvent **à elle**.

▌ - **à** + stressed (disjunctive) personal pronoun with a very few verbs,
such as **penser**, **renoncer**, **songer**

▶ Verbs with object:
see p. 135

Tu veux parler **de ta femme** ? – Non, je ne veux pas parler **d'elle**.

▌ - **de** + stressed (disjunctive) personal pronoun.

Fixed Expressions with *y* and *en*

Ça **y** est.	*That's it. / There you are.*
Je n'**y** tiens plus.	*I can't stand it any longer.*
Vous **y** êtes ?	*Are you ready?*
Je n'**y** peux rien. /	
Je n'**y** suis pour rien.	*I can't help it.*
Vas-**y**.	*Let's go. / You go.*
Il **y** a deux heures, ...	*Two hours ago ...*
Il **y** a des gens qui...	*There are people who ...*
Il **y** a des pommes ?	*Are there any apples?*
Non, il n'**y** en a plus.	*No, there aren't any more.*
J'**en** ai pour une seconde.	*I'll be right back.*
Où **en** étions-nous restés ?	*Where did we stop / leave off?*
J'**en** ai eu pour mille euros.	*It cost me 1000 euros.*
J'**en** ai assez.	*That's enough. / I've had enough.*
Ne vous **en** faites pas.	*Don't worry about it.*
Je n'**en** peux plus.	*I can't keep on.*

Placement of Object and Adverbial Pronouns

1. I didn't say it to him / her. 2. There aren't any more.
3. Give it to him / her. 4. Give me one (of them).

Position in a Declarative or Interrogative Sentence

The object and adverbial pronouns precede the conjugated verb.
In a negated sentence, one element of negation (**ne**) comes before
the pronoun, and the other element of negation (such as **pas**)
follows the conjugated verb.

> The placement of the pronouns is strictly regulated in French.

> Tu connais Yves ? – Non, je ne **le** connais pas.
> La semaine dernière, je **lui** ai prêté ma BMW mais
> il ne **me l'**a pas rendu**e**.
> Tu veux dire que tu **la lui** as prêté**e** sans sécurité ?

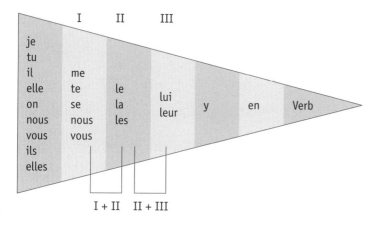

Two object pronouns can be combined only if one of them is **le**, **la**, **les**.

Thus, possible combinations are I + II and II + III.

The adverbial pronouns **y** and **en** can be combined as you wish, with **y** always preceding **en**.

me, **te**, **se**, **nous**, **vous** cannot be combined with **lui** or **leur**. Instead of **lui** or **leur**, the stressed (disjunctive) pronouns are used: **à lui**, **à elle**, **à eux**, or **à elles**.

> Ton chef t'a présenté **au ministre** ? – Oui, il m'a présenté **à lui**.
> Et il t'a présenté aussi **à sa femme** ? – Oui, il m'a présenté aussi **à elle**.

Position in a Declarative or Interrogative Sentence with an Infinitive Following

If the object or adverbial pronouns refer to an infinitive, they directly precede the infinitive.

> Est-ce qu'on va montrer **les photos à Yvette** ?
> – Oui, on va **les lui** montrer.

> Est-ce qu'il faut **lui** offrir **du café** ?
> – Oui, mais on ne va **lui en** offrir qu'une tasse.

With some verbs, the pronoun does not refer to the infinitive but to the preceding main verb. These include **voir**, **regarder**, **entendre**, **écouter**, **sentir**, **laisser**, **faire**, **envoyer**. Here the pronouns are placed before the conjugated verb.

> **Les enfants** ont crié très fort. – Tu **les** as entendus crier ?
> **La moto** de Jean était en panne. – Mais il **l'**a fait réparer.

Position in an Imperative Sentence

> ! Before **en**, **moi**, and **toi**, change to **m'** and **t'** (m'en, t'en).

With the affirmative imperative, the pronouns are attached to the verb by a hyphen. The direct object pronoun is placed before the indirect object pronoun.
Y and **en** are always in final position. Note: Instead of **me** and **te**, use **moi** and **toi**.

Tu prends du beurre ? – Oui, passe-**le-moi**.
Tu veux du vin ? – Oui, donne-**m'en** un verre.

With the negative imperative, the rules are identical to those for a declarative sentence.

> J'aimerais que tu restes ! Ne **t'en** va pas.
> Ne **me** regarde pas comme ça.

1. Answer Monsieur Dutour. Replace the words in bold with **y** and **en**. *

a) Quand est-ce que vous allez **à Marseille** ? (nous – dans quinze jours)

   Nous y allons dans quinze jours.

b) A quelle heure vous arriverez **à la gare** ? (nous – à 14 heures 25)

   _____

c) Vous avez déjà parlé **de ce voyage** au chef ? (je – la semaine dernière)

   _____

d) Vous pensez déjà **à ce voyage** ? (je)

   _____

e) Vous allez monter **sur la colline de la basilique Notre-Dame-de-la-Garde** ? (nous)

   _____

f) Pourriez-vous acheter **deux bouteilles de Pastis** ? (je)

   _____

2. Fill in the blanks with **y** or **en**. *

a) Philippe, vas- __y__ .

b) Vous prenez du lait dans votre café ? – Non, je n' _____ prends pas.

c) Avez-vous encore du café ? – Oui, j' _____ ai.

d) Il _____ a encore quelques tartelettes.

e) J' _____ prends une, merci.

f) Il faut que je m'_____ aille maintenant.

g) Ne partez pas ! Restez-_____ .

> y – y – y
> en – en – en

Adverbial Pronouns y *and* en

3. Answer the questions. Replace the parts of the sentences in **bold** with the appropriate personal pronouns and with **y** or **en**. **

a) Est-ce que tu as vu **ta sœur** ?

Non, _____je ne l'ai pas vue_____ .

b) Et tu n'as pas vu **ton frère** non plus ?

Si, _____ .

c) Vous allez **en ville** demain ?

Oui, _____ .

d) Tu diras bonjour **à ton frère** ?

Oui, _____ .

e) Tu vas téléphoner **à ta sœur** prochainement ?

Oui, _____ .

f) Est-ce que tu penses souvent **à ta sœur** ?

Non, _____ .

g) Elle travaille toujours **chez Peugeot** ?

Non, _____ .

h) Et son mari, il s'intéresse toujours **aux voitures** ?

Non, _____ .

i) Il ne travaille plus **au garage** ?

Non, _____ .

beau-frère –
brother-in-law

j) La maison appartient toujours **à ta sœur et à ton beau-frère** ?

Oui, _____ .

k) Ils ont changé **de voiture** ?

Non, _____ .

l) Ils n'ont pas besoin **de ta mère** ?

Non, _____ .

m) Et ta sœur, elle n'a pas aidé **votre mère** ?

Si, _____ .

Stressed (Disjunctive) Personal Pronouns: *moi, toi...*

Yvette va au restaurant.
①

Et Yves ?
② Lui aussi.

Et les voisins ?
③ Eux aussi.

1. Yvette is going to the restaurant. 2. And Yves ?-- He is too. 3. And the neighbors? – They are too.

Forms

	1st Person	2nd Person	3rd Person Masculine	Feminine
Singular	**moi**	**toi**	**lui**	**elle**
Plural	**nous**	**vous**	**eux**	**elles**

Use

The stressed, or disjunctive, personal pronouns can only take the place of persons, in these cases:

Qui est-ce qui veut aller chez les Dutour ?
Michel: Pas **moi.**
Isabelle: **Moi** non plus.

- in sentences without a verb.

> This also applies to compounds with **et**, **ou**, **ni... ni**, etc.

Thierry: Je ne veux pas aller **chez eux.**
Florence: Michel, tu viens **avec moi** ?

- after prepositions.

Voilà une photo des Dutour.
C'est elle qui crie sans arrêt.
Et **ce sont eux** que mon grand-père n'a jamais aimés.

- after **c'est** and **ce sont.**

Et c'est lui qui est beaucoup plus intelligent **qu'elle.**

- after **que** in comparisons.

Toi, tu vas nous accompagner et **toi, tu** vas rester à la maison.

- to place emphasis on persons, as in colloquial speech.

Stressed (Disjunctive) Personal Pronouns

1. Replace the words in **bold** with the appropriate stressed personal pronouns. *

a) Thierry : Je ne veux pas aller **chez les Dutour**.   _____chez eux_____

b) Florence : Tu peux venir **avec Michel**.   _____

c) Thierry : Non, je ne vais pas **avec toi et Michel**.   _____

d) Michel : Je suis d'accord **avec Florence**.   _____

e) Florence : Je n'ai pas envie d'y aller **avec mes amies**.   _____

f) Thierry : Alors, on va au cinéma **avec mes amis**.   _____

2. Translate the following. **

a) Thierry and I are not going to the Dutours' house.

   Thierry et moi, nous n'allons pas chez les Dutour.

b) He doesn't want to go with him either.

   _____

c) And Florence isn't going with them either.

   _____

to agree, be in
agreement –
être d'accord

d) And he agrees with her.

   _____

to argue, quarrel –
se disputer

e) And she doesn't want to argue with him.

   _____

f) Everybody is unwilling to go to their house.

   _____

Demonstrative Pronouns

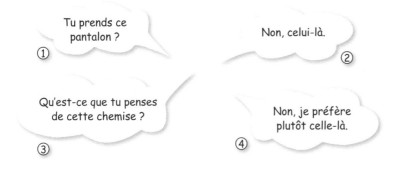

1. Are you taking these pants? 2. No, those. 3. What do you think of this shirt?
4. No, I prefer that one instead.

Celui, celle ...

Forms

	Masculine	Feminine
Singular	celui	celle
Plural	ceux	celles

Use

Celui, **celle**, **ceux**, and **celles** are never used alone.

Quelle voiture est-ce que je prends pour aller en ville ?
– Prends **celle de** Michel.

Either they are followed by a complement with a preposition
(usually **de**, **à**, or **pour**) ...

Je voudrais un chou-fleur. – Prenez **celui que** vous préférez.
                                                                     chou-fleur – *cauliflower*

- or a relative clause (with **qui**, **que**, **dont**, or **où**).

Qu'est-ce que je mets comme verres ?
Ceux-ci ou **ceux-là** ? – Plutôt **ceux-là**.
Et comme serviettes ? – Prends **celles-ci**.

In a choice between two things, **celui-ci** points to the one that
was mentioned first or is closer; **celui-là** refers to the one mentioned
second or farther away.

In literary French, **ça** is replaced by **cela**.

cela, *ça*, and *ce*

> Ça te plaît ?

> Oui, c'est super.

Do you like it? – Yes, it's super.

Use

Ça va ? – Oui, **ça** va mieux.
« Computer », **ça** ne se dit pas en français.

Ça usually is used when **il** could lead to confusion with a person.

La Polynésie française, **c'est** magnifique.
Voilà mes livres. – Non, **ce sont** mes livres.

Ce and **c'** are used before **être**.

1. Thierry and Florence are in a department store. Fill in the blanks with the missing demonstrative pronouns. *

a) F. : Alors, tu veux acheter un pantalon. Prends _celui-là._

b) T. : Moi, je préfère _____ qui se trouve à côté.

c) F. : Voilà les chemises. J'en ai trouvé une belle. Que penses-tu

     de _____ ?

d) T. : _____ aux manches courtes me plaît plus.

e) F. : Tu as vu les chaussures ? Qu'est-ce que tu préfères ? _____ ou

     _____ ?

f) T. : J'aimerais prendre _____ dont je t'ai parlé hier.

g) F. : On achète encore une cravate. Prends _____ où il y a toutes

     sortes de papillons.

h) T. : Il me faudrait encore un pull. _____ ou _____ ?

i) F. : J'adore _____ à col roulé.

j) T : Regarde ces slips. Tu préfères _____ ou _____ ?

k) F : _____ est plus sexy.

Possessive Pronouns

---

1. Is this your desk? – Yes, it's mine. 2. And these sheets of paper?
Do they belong to you? – Yes, they're mine.

Forms

	Masculine	Feminine	Masculine	Feminine
	A qui est ce bureau ?	Et cette chaise ?	Et ces crayons ?	Et ces feuilles ?
Singular	C'est	C'est	Ce sont	Ce sont
1st Person	**le mien**	**la mienne**	**les miens**	**les miennes**
2nd Person	**le tien**	**la tienne**	**les tiens**	**les tiennes**
3rd Person	**le sien.**	**la sienne.**	**les siens.**	**les siennes.**
Plural	C'est	C'est	Ce sont	Ce sont
1st Person	**le nôtre**	**la nôtre**	**les nôtres**	**les nôtres**
2nd Person	**le vôtre**	**la vôtre**	**les vôtres**	**les vôtres**
3rd Person	**le leur.**	**la leur.**	**les leurs.**	**les leurs.**

The possessive pronouns, like the possessive determiners, agree in number and gender with the associated noun.

▶ Possessive determiners: see p. 31

If two owners or possessors are mentioned, one is placed before the noun as a possessive determiner, and the other is placed after it as a possessive pronoun.

mes amis et **les tiens**...   *my friends and yours ...*

1. Answer all the questions in the affirmative. Use the appropriate possessive pronouns. *

a) C'est votre voiture?

   Oui, c'est la mienne.   .

b) Et ce vélo ?

C'est _____ .

c) Et ces meubles ?

Ce sont _____ .

d) Et ces photos ?

_____ .

e) Ce sont les livres de votre fille ?

Oui, _____ .

f) Et ces CD ? Ils sont à votre fils ?

_____ .

g) Cette maison est à vous et votre femme ?

_____ .

h) Et ces deux voitures ?

_____ .

i) Ce sont les jouets de vos enfants ?

Oui, _____ .

j) Et ces guitares ?

_____ .

k) Et cette moto ? Elle est à votre mère ?

Oui, _____ .

l) C'est la bicyclette de votre père ?

Oui, _____ .

Indefinite Pronouns: *tout, chacun, plusieurs, certains*

1. *Last week I celebrated my birthday with my friends.* 2. *They all were there.*
3. *Each one brought a little gift.* 4. *Several came with their girlfriends.*
5. *And some stayed until the next morning.*

Tous, toutes – chacun, chacune

▶ On "tout" as a determiner, see p. 35

Use

La semaine dernière, mes amis sont venus.
– Il y avait beaucoup d'amis ?
Oui, **tous** sont venus.
– Et les filles ?
Elles étaient **toutes** là.

Tous and **toutes** agree in gender with the associated noun and refer to all the persons or things in a group. In the examples above, **tous** and **toutes** refer to the subject.

Je t'ai déjà montré les films ? – Oui, tu me **les** avais montrés **tous**.
Et les photos ? Tu les connais déjà ? – Oui, je **les** connais **toutes**.

Here **tous** and **toutes** refer to a direct object. In these cases, the object pronoun **les** precedes the conjugated verb.

Tous les films sont rangés dans le placard.
Chacun a sa place bien précise.
Et les photos, je vais les coller dans un album.
Chacune doit être commentée par un petit texte.

Chacun and **chacune** agree in gender with the associated noun and refer to each and every person or thing in a group.

le placard – *closet, cupboard*

Chacun and **chacune** have no plural forms. **!**

Chez moi, **tout** doit être correct.

Tout is invariable and refers to a totality.

Tout is the equivalent of "everything, all."

Tout ce qui est à la mode me plaît.
Tout ce qu'on veut acheter se trouve dans ce centre commercial.
Tous ceux qui sont venus reviendront l'année prochaine.
Et **tous ceux que** j'ai rencontrés ont été bien contents.

After the pronouns **tout**, **tous**, and **toutes**, a relative clause cannot be directly attached. Before a relative clause, **tout** must be followed by **ce**, and **tous** and **toutes** must be followed by **ceux** or **celles**.

Tout is flexible; it can be an adjective, an adverb, and a noun, as well as a pronoun.

Plusieurs – certains

Plusieurs de mes amis habitent à Paris.

Some of my friends live in Paris.

Certains is used above all in literary French.

Plusieurs and **certains**... are not only determiners but can also serve as pronouns.

Use

Ce matin, j'ai acheté des bananes. **Plusieurs** sont déjà abîmées.

Plusieurs can refer to things and persons.

abîmé – *spoiled, ruined*

En ce moment, les économistes discutent beaucoup de la situation actuelle. **Certains** ne pensent pas que l'économie reprenne.

Certains refers only to persons.

Practice and Application

Indefinite Pronouns

1. Fill in the blanks with the appropriate indefinite pronouns of **tout**. *

a) La semaine dernière mes amis sont venus. __Tous__ étaient là.

b) Il y avait aussi des filles. Tu les connais _____ ? – Non !

c) _____ celles qui sont venues reviendront la semaine prochaine.

d) J'ai préparé aussi un repas. Ils ont presque _____ mangé.

le gaspillage –
wastefulness, waste
la nourriture –
food (in general),
nourishment

e) _____ ce qui restait, je l'ai mangé le lendemain.

f) Et mes amis sont presque _____ contre le gaspillage de la nourriture.

2. Translate the following, using the indefinite determiners and pronouns of **tout** and / or **chaque**. ***

a) Do all these cassettes belong to you? – No, they all belong to my sister.

   ___Toutes ces cassettes sont à toi ?_____

   _____

b) Did you wash the pants? – Yes, I washed them all. Each pair of pants has to be washed separately.

   _____

   _____

to wash – laver
to shine, gleam – briller

c) For the party I have to wash every single plate. They all have to shine. And each one has to be put in its exact place.

   _____

   _____

d) Have all the children gone home? – No, not all. But every child has to be home at eight o'clock.

   _____

   _____

e) Did you eat everything? – No, not everything. But we will eat all the leftovers tomorrow.

   _____

   _____

f) He slept all day. He does that every day.

   _____

Relative Pronouns

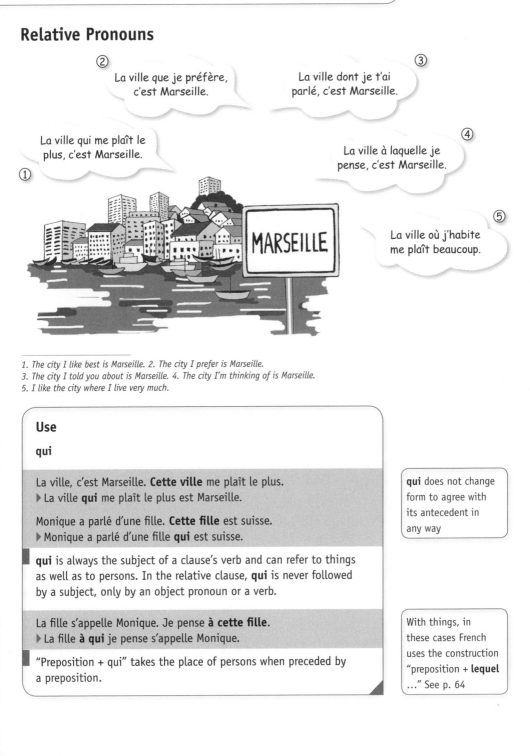

② La ville que je préfère, c'est Marseille.

③ La ville dont je t'ai parlé, c'est Marseille.

① La ville qui me plaît le plus, c'est Marseille.

④ La ville à laquelle je pense, c'est Marseille.

⑤ La ville où j'habite me plaît beaucoup.

MARSEILLE

1. The city I like best is Marseille. 2. The city I prefer is Marseille.
3. The city I told you about is Marseille. 4. The city I'm thinking of is Marseille.
5. I like the city where I live very much.

Use

qui

La ville, c'est Marseille. **Cette ville** me plaît le plus.
▶ La ville **qui** me plaît le plus est Marseille.

Monique a parlé d'une fille. **Cette fille** est suisse.
▶ Monique a parlé d'une fille **qui** est suisse.

qui is always the subject of a clause's verb and can refer to things as well as to persons. In the relative clause, **qui** is never followed by a subject, only by an object pronoun or a verb.

La fille s'appelle Monique. Je pense **à cette fille**.
▶ La fille **à qui** je pense s'appelle Monique.

"Preposition + qui" takes the place of persons when preceded by a preposition.

> **qui** does not change form to agree with its antecedent in any way

> With things, in these cases French uses the construction "preposition + **lequel** ..." See p. 64

que

La ville, c'est Marseille. Je préfère **Marseille**.
▶ La ville **que** je préfère, c'est Marseille. *(The city that ...)*

█ **que** always takes the place of the direct object (accusative object) of a clause and can refer to things or to persons. A subject always follows **que**.

dont

La ville, c'est Marseille. Je t'ai parlé **de Marseille**.
▶ La ville **dont** je t'ai parlé, c'est Marseille. *(The city about which ...)*

Le monsieur s'appelle Dutour. J'ai vu la fille **de ce monsieur**.
▶ Le monsieur **dont** j'ai vu la fille s'appelle Dutour.
  (The gentleman whose ...)

█ **dont** takes the place of a complement with **de** and can also refer to persons or to things. It has no effect on word order.

lequel, laquelle, lesquels, lesquelles

La ville, c'est Marseille. Je pense **à cette ville**.
▶ La ville **à laquelle** je pense, c'est Marseille. *(... of which / about which ...)*

Nous avons vu des touristes. **Parmi les touristes** se trouvaient deux Japonais.
▶ Nous avons vu des touristes **parmi lesquels** se trouvaient deux Japonais. *(... among whom ...)*

█ The construction "preposition + **lequel**" takes the place of complements with a preposition (**à**, **de**, **pour**, **avec**, **dans** ...). With things, this construction is required. With persons, it is used only in literary French; otherwise, "preposition + **qui**" is used. In most cases, **dont** also can be used in place of **de** + **lequel**...

! Exception: After **parmi** and **entre**, only **lequel**... can be used!

où

Ce pays me plaît beaucoup. Je suis allée **dans ce pays**.
▶ Le pays **où** je suis allée me plaît beaucoup. *(The country where / to which …)*

Je me rappelle bien de ce soir-là. **Le soir** nous sommes allés au cinéma.
▶ Je me rappelle bien du soir **où** nous sommes allés au cinéma. *(… on the evening on which …)*

The pronoun **où** has the function of a place determination.
It can also be used for time when preceded by expressions such as **le jour**, **le soir**, **le mois**, etc. It is also used after **à l'époque** and **au moment**.

ce qui, ce que

Je ne sais pas **ce qui** lui plaît. *(I don't know what …)*

ce qui (as subject) and **ce que** (as direct object) are the equivalent of "what."

▶ On **tout / tous** in connection with relative clauses, see p. 61

Practice and Application

Relative Pronouns

1. Choose between **qui** and **que**. *

a) La ville _qui_ me plaît le plus, c'est Marseille.

b) C'est la ville _____ je préfère.

c) Les enfants de Monsieur Dutour, c'est Nicole _____ a treize ans,

Benjamin _____ a onze ans, et Olivier _____ a cinq ans.

d) Benjamin _____ je ne connais pas est un garçon bien sage.

e) Jean a parlé d'une fille _____est suisse.

f) Et la fille _____ j'aime est portugaise.

2. Link the clauses below with **dont**. **

a) Les Dutour ont trois enfants. Deux de ces enfants sont des garçons.

Les Dutour ont trois enfants dont deux sont des garçons.

b) La fille est suisse. Jean a parlé de cette fille.

_____

c) La ville s'appelle Marseille. Nous avons vu un film de cette ville.

_____

d) Voilà Emma et Fanny. La passion de ces deux filles est la nourriture.

_____

_____

e) J'ai vu une fille. Ses parents habitent au Portugal.

_____

3. Fill in the blanks with the appropriate relative pronouns. ***

a) Je ne connais personne ____qui____ sache parler le japonais.

b) La femme _____ je t'ai parlé la semaine dernière est morte par accident.

le metteur en scène – *director*

l'amant – *lover*

c) Connaissez-vous le metteur en scène _____ a fait le film « L'Amant » ?

d) C'est un livre _____ personne ne peut résister.

les jumelles – *binoculars*

e) Je ne trouve plus les jumelles _____ s'est servi mon grand-père.

f) La ville _____ je rêve s'appelle Marseille.

66

g) La personne _____ je tiens beaucoup est ma mère.

h) L'arc-en-ciel _____ je regarde est en train de disparaître.

l'arc-en-ciel – rainbow

i) La personne _____ je crois le plus est mon patron.

j) Le pays _____ j'aimerais vivre c'est la France.

k) Voilà la raison pour _____ elle est partie.

l) Les personnes parmi _____ se trouve M. Dutour jouent toutes d'un instrument de musique.

m) Ce sont des événements _____ les Allemands penseront encore dans 20 ans.

4. Translate the following, using the relative pronouns.

a) The city where I live is named San Francisco.

   La ville où j'habite s'appelle San Francisco.

b) Is there a city that you prefer?

   _____

c) No, San Francisco is the city that I like best.

   _____

d) My wife, who is 38 years old, comes from New York City.

   _____

e) New York City, which is more famous than San Francisco, is the city that my wife likes best.

   _____

   _____

f) My wife's son, whom everyone calls Dodo, was born in Chicago.

   _____

   _____

g) My girlfriend's daughter, who is 25 years old, is studying in Dallas.

   _____

   _____

The Verb

Tense

1. Time of Speaking

Only the most commonly used tenses are dealt with in this book. Forms that are used primarily in literary French (such as the past anterior and the imperfect subjunctive) are disregarded here.

A verb not only states when something happens and for how long, but it also places this occurrence in a temporal relationship to the speaker or narrator.

Thus a certain event may happen before, during, or after the time at which someone is speaking about it. Particular tenses are associated with each of the three times.

Time of Speaking		
Event		
before	**simultaneously**	**after**
compound past **imperfect**	**present**	**simple future** **near future**

Ma femme **est** dans la cuisine. Elle **prépare** le repas.

ongoing at the time of speaking: **present**

Pendant que je **travaillais** à l'ordinateur, quelqu'un **a frappé** à la porte.

before the time of speaking: **imperfect, compound past**

Nos enfants sont partis. Ils **vont revenir** tout de suite.
Demain, ils **iront** en ville.

after the time of speaking: **near future** or **simple future**

2. Time of Storytelling

If someone is telling a story, he places himself in the past. Here too, an event that is recounted can occur before, at the same time as, or after the moment in which the narrator places himself.

Point of Departure of Story		
Event		
before	**simultaneously**	**after**
pluperfect	imperfect compound past	conditional

Il **avait** faim. Il **savait** qu'il n'**avait** plus d'argent.
Tout à coup, quelqu'un **a frappé** à la porte.

at the same time as the storytelling: **imperfect** or **compound past**

▶ Imperfect, see p. 92

Il **avait dépensé** tout son argent.
Il n'**avait** pas **arrêté** d'acheter des livres et des CD.

before the storytelling: **pluperfect**

▶ Compound past,
see p. 83

Et il savait que la faim **serait** encore plus grande et qu'il ne **changerait** jamais.

after the storytelling: **conditional**

▶ Pluperfect,
see p. 97

▶ Conditional,
see p. 113

Mood

> Je souhaite qu'il apprenne le français.

I wish he would learn French.

A verb form can do more than give information about the time of speaking or of telling a story; it can also express a personal attitude toward an event. This is known as the grammatical mood.

If a fact is expressed, the **future** is used.

> Ma femme dit que nos amis **viendront**.
> *My wife says that our friends are coming.*

If a wish is expressed, use the **subjunctive**.

> Ma femme dit que nos amis **viennent**.
> *My wife says that our friends should come.*

If a fact is involved, use the **present**.

> Vous avez fait votre choix ?   Oui, je **prends** le menu à cent euros.
> ("I'll take / have …")

To express a polite request, use the **conditional**.

> Vous avez fait votre choix ?   Oui, je **voudrais** le menu à 15 euros.
> ("I'd like to have …")
>
> **Pourriez**-vous m'aider s.v.p. ?   *Could you help me, please?*

With commands, the **imperative** is used.

> « Asseyez-vous, s'il vous plaît. »   *"Sit down, please."*
> « Attends-moi. »   *"Wait for me."*

Present Tense

« Le lundi, le mardi, le mercredi, le jeudi, le vendredi et le samedi, je regarde la télé. »

1. Qu'est-ce qu'il fait dimanche ?   – Il fait la vaisselle.
2. Qu'est-ce qu'il fait normalement ? – Il regarde la télé.

1. What is he doing this Sunday? – He's doing the dishes.
2. What does he normally do? – He watches television.

Formation of the Present

In the present tense, verbs have different endings, depending on which group they belong to:

	Group 1: Verbs ending in **-er**	Group 2: Verbs ending in **-ir** (type: finir) **-ir**	Group 3: Irregular verbs! Verbs ending in … **-ir**	**-oir**	**-re**
Singular					
je	-e	-is	-s/-e	-s/-x	-s/-s
tu	-es	-is	-s/-es	-s/-x	-s/-s
il/elle/on	-e	-it	-t/-e	-t/-d	-t/-d
Plural					
nous	-ons	-issons	-ons	-ons	-ons
vous	-ez	-issez	-ez	-ez	-ez
ils/elles	-ent	-issent	-ent	-ent	-ent

> You will find the most important irregular verbs in the list on pp. 74–79.

The ending of the present tense for **vous** is the most regular form. With three exceptions, all verbs end in **-ez** here.

These exceptions are:

être - vous êtes   **dire** - vous dites   **faire** - vous faites

71

Use

Elle **travaille** dans le jardin.
En ce moment, les enfants **jouent** dans leur chambre.

▌ The present is used for events occurring at the present moment ...

Je **joue** au tennis le samedi soir.
Une fois par semaine, on **va** au restaurant.

▌ – habitual occurrences ...

La lune **tourne** autour de la terre.
Trois et trois **font** six.

▌ – general truths and concepts ...

La télé **marche** depuis ce matin.
Cela fait cinq ans que je ne **fume** plus.

▌ – events begun in the past and not yet completed ...

Il **sort** du supermarché.
Le train **part**.

▌ – events that have just taken place (in place of the construction "Il vient de sortir du supermarché").

Nous **partons** en voyage demain.
On **mange** quelque chose à midi ?

▌ The present can also be used with intended events in the future. Such sentences must contain expressions of time such as **demain**, **à midi**. Usually these are to take place in the near future.

S'il **vient** demain, je serai content.
Si on ne **mange** pas trop, on se sent bien.

▶ For information on **si** clauses, see p. 131

▌ If there is a possibility that a condition can be fulfilled, the present tense is used in the **si** clause.

Overview of Verbs in the Present

A verb is always made up of a stem and an ending. Every verb has at least one verb stem.

> Example: **vous aimez**
> Stem: **aim-**   Ending: **-ez**.

1. Verbs Ending in -er (Group 1)

Approximately 90% of French verbs end in **-er**.

Verbs ending in **-er**: aimer

j'aim**e**	nous aim**ons**
tu aim**es**	vous aim**ez**
il aim**e**	ils aim**ent**

A number of verbs ending in **-er** change their verb stem. They can be broken down into various subgroups:

Verbs ending in **-eler** or **-eter**: appeler

j'appe**lle**	nous appelons
tu appe**lles**	vous appelez
il appe**lle**	ils appe**llent**

<u>also</u>: épeler, étiqueter, jeter, renouveler, se rappeler

Verbs ending in **-e(...)er**: acheter

j'ach**è**te	nous achetons
tu ach**è**tes	vous achetez
il ach**è**te	ils ach**è**tent

<u>also</u>: amener, emmener, enlever, geler, lever, modeler, peler, peser, se promener, semer

Verbs ending in **-é(...)er**: espérer

j'esp**è**re	nous espérons
tu esp**è**res	vous espérez
il esp**è**re	ils esp**è**rent

<u>also</u>: céder, exagérer, posséder, préférer, protéger, répéter, s'inquiéter

---

Verbs ending in **-ger**: manger

je mange	nous mang**e**ons
tu manges	vous mangez
il mange	ils mangent

<u>also</u>: changer, corriger, déranger, diriger, interroger, ranger, s'allonger

---

Verbs ending in **-cer**: commencer

je commence	nous commen**ç**ons
tu commences	vous commencez
il commence	ils commencent

<u>also</u>: annoncer, avancer, lancer, prononcer, remplacer

Verbs ending in **-oyer**, **-uyer**, **-ayer**: nettoyer

je nettoie	nous nettoyons
tu nettoies	vous nettoyez
il nettoie	ils nettoient

<u>also</u>: employer, essayer, essuyer, payer, s'ennuyer, se noyer, tutoyer

> ❗ With verbs ending in **-ayer**, there are two possible spellings: je **paie** or je **paye**

2. Verbs Ending in -ir: *finir* Type (Group 2):

Verbs ending in **-ir**: finir

je finis	nous finissons
tu finis	vous finissez
il finit	ils finissent

<u>also</u>: agir, choisir, nourrir, punir, ralentir, réagir, réfléchir, réussir, saisir

3. Irregular Verbs (Group 3):

> **Study tip:**
> These three verbs are especially important, since they are required in the formation of several other tenses.

avoir	être	aller
j'ai	je suis	je vais
tu as	tu es	tu vas
il/elle/on a	il/elle/on est	il/elle/on va
nous avons	nous sommes	nous allons
vous avez	vous êtes	vous allez
ils/elles ont	ils/elles sont	ils/elles vont

Overview of Verbs in the Present

> About 200 French verbs are conjugated irregularly. Many of them are part of the essential vocabulary!

acquérir

j'acquiers	nous acquérons	<u>also</u>: (re)conquérir,
il acquiert	ils acquièrent	requérir

s'asseoir

je m'assois	nous asseyons	<u>imperative</u>: assieds-toi,
il s'assoit	ils s'assoient	asseyez-vous

battre

je bats	nous battons	<u>also</u>: abattre,
il bat	ils battent	combattre

boire

je bois	nous buvons
il boit	ils boivent

conclure

je conclus	nous concluons	<u>also</u>: exclure,
il conclut	ils concluent	inclure

conduire

je conduis	nous conduisons	<u>also</u>: construire, cuire,
il conduit	ils conduisent	déduire, détruire, instruire, luire, nuire, produire, réduire, traduire

connaître

je connais	nous connaissons	<u>also</u>: apparaître,
il connaît	ils connaissent	disparaître, paraître, reconnaître

courir

je cours	nous courons	<u>also</u>: concourir, parcourir
il court	ils courent	

craindre

je crains	nous craignons	<u>also</u>: contraindre,
il craint	ils craignent	plaindre, atteindre, éteindre, peindre, joindre, rejoindre

croire

je crois	nous croyons
il croit	ils croient

devoir

je dois	nous devons
il doit	ils doivent

dire

> ! But: vous contredisez, vous interdisez

je dis	nous disons	also: contredire, interdire
tu dis	vous dites	
il dit	ils disent	

dormir

je dors	nous dormons	also: endormir
il dort	ils dorment	

écrire

j'écris	nous écrivons	also: décrire, inscrire,
il écrit	ils écrivent	prescrire, souscrire,
		transcrire

faire

je fais	nous faisons	also: défaire, satisfaire
tu fais	vous faites	
il fait	ils font	

falloir

il faut

lire

je lis	nous lisons	also: élire, réélire, relire
il lit	ils lisent	

mentir

je mens	nous mentons	also: (res)sentir, (re)partir,
il ment	ils mentent	sortir

mettre

je mets	nous mettons	<u>also</u>: admettre, émettre,
il met	ils mettent	permettre, promettre,
		remettre, transmettre

mourir

je meurs	nous mourons
il meurt	ils meurent

mouvoir

je meus	nous mouvons	<u>also</u>: émouvoir
il meut	ils meuvent	

naître

je nais	nous naissons	<u>also</u>: renaître
il naît	ils naissent	

ouvrir

j'ouvre	nous ouvrons	<u>also</u>: couvrir, découvrir,
il ouvre	ils ouvrent	offrir, souffrir, courir

plaire

je plais	nous plaisons	<u>also</u>: déplaire
il plaît	ils plaisent	

pleuvoir

il pleut

pouvoir

je peux	nous pouvons
tu peux	vous pouvez
il peut	ils peuvent

prendre

je prends	nous prenons	<u>also</u>: apprendre,
il prend	ils prennent	comprendre, entreprendre,
		reprendre, surprendre

recevoir

| je reçois | nous recevons | also: apercevoir, concevoir, décevoir, percevoir |
| il reçoit | ils reçoivent | |

rendre

| je rends | nous rendons | also: attendre, défendre, dépendre, descendre, détendre, entendre, étendre, pendre, prétendre, suspendre, vendre, répandre, confondre, correspondre, fondre, répondre, perdre, mordre, tordre, corrompre, interrompre, rompre |
| il rend | ils rendent | |

résoudre

| je résous | nous résolvons | also: dissoudre |
| il résout | ils résolvent | |

rire

| je ris | nous rions | also: sourire |
| il rit | ils rient | |

savoir

| je sais | nous savons | |
| il sait | ils savent | |

servir

| je sers | nous servons | also: desservir |
| il sert | ils servent | |

suivre

| je suis | nous suivons | also: poursuivre |
| il suit | ils suivent | |

se taire

| je me tais | nous nous taisons | |
| il se tait | ils se taisent | |

tenir

je tiens	nous tenons	<u>also</u>: s'abstenir, apparte-
il tient	ils tiennent	nir, contenir, entretenir,
		maintenir, obtenir, convenir,
		devenir, intervenir, parvenir,
		prévenir, redevenir, retenir,
		revenir, soutenir, se souvenir,
		survenir, venir

vaincre

| je vaincs | nous vainquons | <u>also</u>: convaincre |
| il vainc | ils vainquent | |

valoir

| je vaux | nous valons | <u>also</u>: équivaloir |
| il vaut | ils valent | |

vivre

| je vis | nous vivons | <u>also</u>: survivre |
| il vit | ils vivent | |

voir

| je vois | nous voyons | <u>also</u>: prévoir, revoir |
| il voit | ils voient | |

vouloir

| je veux | nous voulons | |
| il veut | ils veulent | |

Present Tense

1. Write in the missing forms of the present tense and of the infinitive. *

a) tirer   je _tire_   nous _tirons_   ils _tirent_

b) _____   tu _____   nous épelons   elles _____

c) _____   je gèle   vous _____   ils _____

d) mener   elle _____   nous _____   ils _____

e) _____   je préfère   vous _____   elles _____

f) _____   je _____   tu places   nous _____

g) _____   on nage   nous _____   ils _____

h) envoyer   j' _____   nous _____   ils _____

i) _____   je réussis   vous _____   elles _____

j) _____   tu vends   nous _____   ils _____

k) croire   tu _____   nous _____   ils _____

l) _____   tu _____   nous sommes   ils _____

m) _____   tu _____   nous _____   ils ont

2. Fill in the blanks with the missing form of the present tense. **

a) Comme ils _ont_ faim, ils _mangent_ des fruits. (avoir / manger)

b) Quel jour _____-nous ? – On _____ le deux mars. (être / être)

feu d'artifice –
fireworks

c) Les gens, où est-ce qu'ils _____? – Ils _____ le parc
pour mieux voir le feu d'artifice. (aller / traverser)

d) _____-vous. (s'asseoir)

e) _____-moi ces blancs d'œufs en neige. (battre)

f) M. Dutour _____ un homme qui _____. (être / boire)

g) Vous _____ les légumes à feu doux. (cuire)

h) La maison _____ sous la verdure. (disparaître)

i) Il _____ un journal en cinq minutes. (parcourir)

j) Nous _____ la lumière à 22 heures. (éteindre)

k) Ils ne _____ pas en Dieu. (croire)

l) Vous _____ faire attention. (devoir)

m) Normalement nous _____ déjà à 10 heures. (dormir)

n) « falloir » _____ avec deux « l ». (s'écrire)

o) Il _____ les enfants en leur donnant ce qu'ils _____.

   (satisfaire / vouloir)

p) La commune _____ les conseillers municipaux. (élire)

q) Elle ne _____ plus ses jambes. (sentir)

r) Je ne _____ pas qu'ils lisent toute la nuit. (permettre)

s) Elle _____ de rhumatismes. (souffrir)

t) Mon voisin _____ sur ses problèmes. (se taire)

3. Put the words provided together to form a sentence. Conjugate the verb in the present tense. ***

a) vous – apprendre – le français – depuis longtemps

   Vous apprenez le français depuis longtemps.

b) tous les jours – je – recevoir – une lettre de mon oncle

c) le magasin – vendre – tous les vêtements en solde

d) je – se souvenir – de madame Dutour

e) nous – vivre – une époque difficile

4. Fill in the missing words. **

Un groupe de jeunes _____est_____ en train de discuter. (être)

Michel: Tu _____ cette phrase en allemand ? (me traduire)

Ahmed: Non, je _____. Cette traduction _____

   Je _____ un roman et je _____ de me parler

   tout le temps. (ne pas vouloir / ne pas plaire / lire / vous interdire)

Sabine: On _____ les autres pour boire un coup ? (rejoindre)

Present Tense

Ahmed: Je _____ mais je _____ de faim.

Peut-être que les autres _____ préparer un repas.

(ne pas avoir soif / mourir / vouloir)

Sabine: Je _____. Il _____ sans arrêt et

sûrement qu'ils _____ aujourd'hui. (ne pas croire /

pleuvoir / ne pas vouloir sortir)

Michel: Alors, qu'est-ce qu'on _____ maintenant ? (faire)

Sabine: Nous _____. Nous _____ au bar du coin.

Et là, nous _____ des sandwichs. (descendre / aller /

manger)

Ahmed: Voilà, pour une fois, tu _____ une bonne idée. Mais

j' _____ seulement à une condition : Je

_____ ton problème de traduction ! (avoir / accepter /

ne pas résoudre)

5. What am I doing at the moment? Translate the following.

a) I'm writing a letter to my friend.

   J'écris une lettre à mon ami.

b) He is 25 years old.

c) He is studying in Paris.

d) He often drinks red wine.

e) He lives alone.

Compound Past and Past Participle

1. Pascal left Paris ten years ago. 2. But this morning I saw him on the street.
3. He has come to see his sister.

Formation

The compound past, or passé composé, is made up of the present tense
of **avoir** or **être** and the past participle.

j'	ai	dormi	**je**	suis	venu(e)
tu	as	dormi	**tu**	es	venu(e)
il	a	dormi	**il**	est	venu
elle	a	dormi	**elle**	est	venue
on	a	dormi	**on**	est	venu(e)(s)
nous	avons	dormi	**nous**	sommes	venu(e)s
vous	avez	dormi	**vous**	êtes	venu(e)s
ils	ont	dormi	**ils**	sont	venus
elles	ont	dormi	**elles**	sont	venues

1. Past Participle

Regular Forms:

Verbs ending in **-er:** ▶ **-é**

> aim**é**, jet**é**, appel**é**, achet**é**, pel**é**, pes**é**, espér**é**, commenc**é**, mang**é**,
> appuy**é**, nettoy**é**, pay**é**, all**é**

Verbs ending in **-ir:** ▶ **-i**

> fin**i**, dorm**i**, part**i**, ment**i**, serv**i**, sort**i**

Verbs ending in **-re:** ▶ **-u**

atten**du**, bat**tu**, descen**du**, interrom**pu**, per**du**, ren**du**, vain**cu**

Important Irregular Forms

These irregular participles are part of the basic French vocabulary. Take a close look at them!

eu	(avoir)	**assis**	(s'asseoir)
acquis	(acquérir)	**conclu**	(conclure)
bu	(boire)	**connu**	(connaître)
conduit	(conduire)	**craint**	(craindre)
couru	(courir)	**dû**	(devoir)
cru	(croire)	**écrit**	(écrire)
dit	(dire)	**fallu**	(falloir)
fait	(faire)	**mis**	(mettre)
lu	(lire)	**mû**	(mouvoir)
mort	(mourir)	**ouvert**	(ouvrir)
né	(naître)	**plu**	(pleuvoir)
plu	(plaire)	**pu**	(pouvoir)
pris	(prendre)	**résolu**	(résoudre)
reçu	(recevoir)	**su**	(savoir)
ri	(rire)	**suffi**	(suffire)
suivi	(suivre)	**tu**	(se taire)
tenu	(tenir)	**valu**	(valoir)
vécu	(vivre)	**venu**	(venir)
vu	(voir)	**voulu**	(vouloir)
été	(être)		

2. *avoir* or *être*?

The compound past (passé composé) is formed either with **avoir** or with **être**. Most verbs use the auxiliary **avoir** to form the compound past. This also applies to the verbs **avoir** and **être** themselves.

> Hier, on **a dormi** jusqu'à neuf heures.
> Vers dix heures, on **a pris** le petit déjeuner.
> On **a** beaucoup **discuté**.
> Tout à coup, mon mari **a eu** peur.
> Ma fille **a été** à Paris et elle n'**a** pas **téléphoné** depuis trois jours.

courir, marcher, nager, rouler, sauter, voler, voyager

Verbs expressing a type of movement form the compound past with **avoir**.

> Nous **avons marché** toute la journée.
> Michel **a nagé** le 200 mètres.
> L'année dernière, j'**ai voyagé** beaucoup.

Verbs that express a direction of motion form the compound past with **être**.

> Nous **sommes allés** en ville.
> On **est restés** jusqu'à cinq heures.
> Ensuite, on **est revenus** à l'hôtel.
> A six heures, mon frère **est venu**.
> Il **est entré** dans la chambre.
> Puis il **est tombé** par terre.

> aller, arriver, entrer, partir, rester, rentrer, tomber, venir, revenir

Some verbs expressing a direction of motion, depending on their meaning, are linked with **avoir** or **être**:
- with **avoir** when they have a direct object (for example, **les valises**, **le courier**, **la voiture**).
- with **être** in all other cases.

> descendre, monter rentrer, sortir

avoir	être
Elle **a descendu** les valises.	Elle **est descendue** dans la rue.
J'**ai monté** le courrier.	Je **suis monté** vers cinq heures.
Il **a rentré** la voiture au garage.	Il **est rentré** vers minuit.
Elle **a sorti** la voiture du garage.	Hier soir, ma fille **est sortie** avec un garçon.

All reflexive verbs form the compound past with **être**.

> Elle s'**est lavé** les mains.
> Elle s'**est adressée** à la vendeuse.

3. Variability of the Past Participle

Compound past with **être**:

> Je suis arrivé(**e**) à sept heures.
> Tu es arrivé(**e**) à sept heures.
> Il est arriv**é** à sept heures.
> Elle est arriv**ée** à sept heures.
> On est arrivé(**e**)(**s**) à sept heures.
> Nous sommes arrivé(**e**)**s** à sept heures.
> Vous êtes arrivé(**e**)(**s**) à sept heures.
> Ils sont arriv**és** à sept heures.
> Elles sont arriv**ées** à sept heures.

> "On" can stand for "tu," "il," "elle," "nous," "ils," or "elles." The ending of the participle changes accordingly.

The past participle, when linked with **être**, always agrees in gender and number with the subject.

> Different rules apply to reflexive verbs. **!**

85

Compound Past and Past Participle

Compound past with **avoir**:

> J'ai passé **mes vacances** en France.
> Pendant quinze jours, j'ai visité **des villes**.
> J'ai pris **beaucoup de photos**.

The past participle linked with **avoir** does not change in number and gender if the direct object <u>follows</u> the verb.

> Direct objects can be identified by the absence of a preposition (à, de) before them.

It changes only if the verb is <u>preceded</u> by a direct object (in the form of **que**, **la**, **les**, **combien de**, etc.).

> Les vacances **que** j'ai passé**es** ont été magnifiques.
> Quand est-ce que tu as visité les villes de France ?
> – Je **les** ai visité**es** pendant les vacances.
> **Combien de photos** est-ce que tu as pris**es** ?

! Careful: After leur and lui, the past participle is not made to agree because leur and lui are indirect objects (to or for whom?).

Compound past of **reflexive verbs**:

> Nous nous sommes lavé les mains.
> Elle s'est acheté une maison.

The participle does not change if it is <u>followed</u> by a direct object (such as **les mains**, **une maison**). The reflexive pronoun, which is put in front, is then automatically the indirect object.

If the reflexive pronoun is the direct object, however, then the participle does change in form. A reflexive pronoun can be a direct object only when the past participle is not followed by a direct object.

s'évanouir – *to faint*
se rendre à – *to go to*

> Ils se sont lavé**s**.
> Elle s'est évanoui**e**.
> Nous nous sommes levé**s** à sept heures.
> Elles se sont rendu**es** à Marseille.

Some verbs that use **à** to connect an indirect object can also be used reflexively with **se**. Then the reflexive pronoun is an indirect object (dative object), and thus there is no change in the past participle.

se parler – *to talk with each other* (parler à qn)
s'écrire – *to write to each other* (écrire à qn)

> Le chancelier et le président de la République ne se sont pas parlé depuis longtemps.
> Moi et mon frère, nous nous sommes écrit pendant toute notre vie.

Use

Un jour, le facteur **est venu** avec une lettre.
Il **a donné** la lettre à mon père.
D'abord, mon père **a ouvert** la lettre, puis
il nous **a regardés** et il s'**est évanoui**.

The compound past describes an action or series of actions completed in the past. One event follows another. The following questions
can be asked here: "What happened at that time?" – "And then?" –
"And then?"

J'**ai passé** mon bac il y a deux mois.
J'**ai vu** Nicole mardi dernier.

The compound past describes events completed in the past whose
consequences continue to affect the present.

Compound Past and Past Participle

1. Put the infinitives below in the correct group: compound past with **avoir** or with **être**.

> aller, venir, vendre, offrir, être, courir, se taire, pouvoir,
> pleuvoir, rire, tomber, devoir, voyager, arriver, se rendre, s'offrir,
> rentrer, se dire

Infinitive	Compound past with **avoir**
_____	_____
_____	_____
_____	_____
_____	_____
_____	_____
_____	_____
_____	_____
_____	_____
_____	_____

Infinitive	Compound past with **être**
_____	_____
_____	_____
_____	_____
_____	_____
_____	_____
_____	_____
_____	_____
_____	_____

2. A man has come home and is going about his usual routine. Replace the infinitives with the correct forms of the compound past. **

a) Un Monsieur – rentrer à la maison.

   Un monsieur est rentré à la maison.

b) D'abord, il – s'asseoir dans un fauteuil.

c) Il – prendre le journal et il le – lire.

d) Il – commencer à faire son ménage.

e) En faisant les vitres, il – tomber par terre. Mais il – se mettre debout.

f) Il – marcher un peu puis il – descendre sa valise du grenier.

g) Il – appeler un taxi. Vingt minutes plus tard, il – venir.

h) Le monsieur – monter dans le taxi. Et la voiture – rouler.

i) Devant un immeuble, il – ouvrir la porte de la voiture.

j) Puis le monsieur – descendre du taxi et – aller à l'hôpital.

k) Un médecin – arriver. Il – dire bonjour au monsieur.

l) Il l' – examiner.

m) Puis le monsieur – partir. Mais devant l'hôpital, il – retomber.

Compound Past and Past Participle

3. Put this story into the past, using the compound past tense. Pay attention to the endings of the participle. **

a) Un monsieur fait un voyage avec sa femme.

   Un monsieur a fait un voyage avec sa femme.

b) Dans un supermarché, il s'achète un paquet de biscuits. Il les mange.

   _____

   _____

c) Ensuite, il va à une station service et prend 50 litres de super sans plomb.

   _____

   _____

d) Puis, le monsieur et sa femme se promènent dans le champs de maïs d'à côté.

   _____

   _____

e) Ils continuent le voyage. Le monsieur conduit sans arrêt.

   _____

   _____

f) Trois heures plus tard, il a faim. Puis, il lit sur une enseigne : « Chez les Belges ».

   _____

   _____

   _____

g) Le monsieur et sa femme entrent dans ce restaurant.

   _____

h) Une dame vient. Elle leur montre une table à deux.

   _____

   _____

i) Les deux prennent place.

   _____

j) La dame arrive avec la carte. Elle la leur donne.

   _____

k) Le monsieur ouvre la carte, mais rien ne lui plaît.

_____

l) Il jette la carte par terre.

_____

n) Les deux descendent l'escalier et quittent le restaurant sans avoir dit au revoir.

_____

_____

o) La dame se tait. Puis elle rit.

_____

p) Le monsieur et sa femme montent dans la voiture et partent sans avoir rien mangé.

_____

_____

Imperfect

1. Il etait une fois un vieux homme.

2. Tous les jours, il allait dans un parc pour promener son chien.

---

1. Once upon a time there was an old man. 2. Every day, he went to a park to walk his dog.

Formation

The **imperfect** (imparfait) is based on the stem of the first person plural form of the **present** tense. The appropriate endings are attached to this stem, as follows:

nous **fais**ons ▶	je fais**ais**
	tu fais**ais**
	il/elle/on fais**ait**
	nous fais**ions**
	vous fais**iez**
	ils/elles fais**aient**

Almost all verbs follow this rule in forming the **imperfect**.

The only exception is **être**. It uses the stem **ét-** to form the **imperfect**.

j'étais	nous étions
tu étais	vous étiez
il était	ils étaient

Use

The imperfect describes a previous habit or a previous state of being.

Autrefois, les gens **allaient** à l'église.
Les enfants **jouaient** dans la cour.
Tous les soirs, on se **mettait** au lit très tôt.

The imperfect answers these questions:
"What was it like previously?" – "What was going on the entire time?"
"What did people customarily do?"

A six heures, il **faisait** jour.
Les oiseaux **chantaient**.

What was it like at 6 o'clock? It was light, and the birds were singing.

The imperfect does not express here that dawn arrived at 6 o'clock, but that it was already light. The birds were already singing. They may have begun their singing as early as 5 o'clock.

Si j'**étais** riche, je vivrais en Espagne.
Si je **gagnais** au loto, je m'achèterais une belle maison.

If the fulfillment of a condition is unlikely, the imperfect is used in the **si** clause.

▶ On **si** clauses, see p. 131

Compound Past or Imperfect?

Quand j'étais à Paris, j'ai visité la tour Eiffel.

When I was in Paris, I visited the Eiffel Tower.

Whereas the **compound past** is used for events that form a series of actions (scenes in the foreground), the **imperfect** is used to depict the attendant circumstances of an action (background).

J'**étais** dans la rue quand la police **est venue**.

| What was going on at the time? | *I was on the street.* |
| And what happened then? | *The police came.* |

Quand j'**étais** dans la rue, je **regardais** les gens. Tout à coup la police **est venue**.

What was going on at the time?	I was on the street and was looking at the people.
What happened then?	The police came.

se sauver – to run away

Quand la police **est venue**, un homme **s'est sauvé**.

What happened?	The police came.
And then?	A man ran away.

J'**ai sorti** de mon sac à dos le plan de la ville parce que je **voulais** trouver la rue Gambetta.

What happened?	I took the city map out of my backpack.
What was going on at the time?	I wanted to find rue Gambetta.

J'**ai sorti** de mon sac à dos le plan de la ville que j'**ai montré** à un passant.

What happened?	I took the city map out of my backpack.
And what happened then?	I showed it to a passerby.

Comme il **pleuvait** sans arrêt, nous **sommes allés** dans un café.

What was going on at the time?	It was raining nonstop.
And what happened?	We went to a café.

une gifle – smack, slap in the face

Comme j'**ai dit** «idiot» à ce passant, il m'**a donné** une gifle.

What happened?	I called him an idiot.
And what happened then?	He slapped my face.

Quand j'**étais** à Paris, j'**allais** au cinéma.

What did I usually do?	Every time I was in Paris, I went to the movies.

Quand j'**étais** à Paris, je **suis allé** au cinéma.

And what was going on at the time?	I was in Paris.
And what happened?	I went (once) to the movies.

Compare "I was at the movies yesterday" and "I went to the movies yesterday."

Both the compound past and the imperfect frequently are rendered in English with the simple past. The difference between the two main past tenses can be difficult for English speakers to master.

1. Fill in the appropriate forms of the imperfect. *

a) A six heures du matin, il __faisait__ jour. Les oiseaux _____

   déjà. (faire / chanter)

b) La maison d'en face _____ au soleil. (luire)   *luire – to gleam, glow*

c) Comme il ne _____ pas en cette période d'été, les arbres

   _____ soif. Les feuilles se _____ à la chaleur.

   (pleuvoir / avoir / recroqueviller)   *recroqueviller – to wilt*

d) Le vent chaud du sud _____ toute la végétation. Elle

   _____ grise. (dessécher / être)   *dessécher – to shrivel up*

e) Les paysans ne _____ plus d'eau des puits. (tirer)   *puits – well*

f) Tout le monde _____ la même question : Si la pluie ne

   _____ pas bientôt, la végétation serait morte. (se poser /

   revenir)

g) Les gens ne _____ plus dormir la nuit, tellement il

   _____ chaud. (pouvoir / faire)

h) Dans la journée, on n' _____ pas de cris d'enfants. Ils ne

   _____ plus. (entendre / jouer)

i) Mais moi, j' _____ cette période estivale. Je ne   *estivale – summer, summery*

   _____ pas. (aimer / se plaindre)

j) Ma femme et moi, nous _____ de ce temps splendide.

   Nous _____ à l'ombre pour bouquiner toute la   *bouquiner – to read*

   journée. On _____ jusqu'à la rentrée. (profiter / s'installer /

   se reposer)

Practice and Application

2. Decide whether the compound past or the imperfect is required in each of the items below. ***

a) Chaque matin, Nathalie __se levait__ à six heures. Lundi dernier,

elle _____ à dix heures seulement. (se lever / se lever)

b) A Paris, il _____ très chaud. On _____ dans

un café pour boire quelque chose. (faire / aller)

c) D'abord, Monsieur Dutour _____ une bière, puis

il _____ le menu à 25 euros et une carafe de vin rouge,

il _____ et ensuite, il _____ .

(boire / commander / manger / payer)

d) Monsieur Rocher _____ dans la rue de l'Eglise quand

il _____ sa femme. (faire des achats / voir)

e) Pendant toute sa vie, Yvonne _____ au bois de

Vincennes. Un jour, elle y _____ un accident grave.

(se promener / voir)

f) Toute la famille _____ très soif. Ils _____

une heure pour les boissons. (avoir / attendre)

g) Pendant qu'il _____ le repas, quelqu'un

_____ à la porte. (préparer / frapper)

h) D'abord les copains _____ au cinéma, puis ils

_____ un verre dans un café. (aller / prendre)

i) Je _____ dans la maison et je _____ le

ménage quand les invités _____ . (être / faire / venir)

se brosser les dents –
to brush one's teeth

j) Tous les jours elle se _____ les dents mais ce jour-là, elle

_____ de le faire. (brosser / oublier)

Pluperfect

Tu as pu parler à Romain?

Non, quand je suis arrivé, il était déjà parti.

1. Were you able to talk to Romain? 2. No, when I arrived, he had already left.

Formation

The pluperfect is made up of the imperfect of **avoir** or **être** and the past participle.

▸ On the use of avoir or être, see the section on the compound past, starting on p. 84

j'	avais	travaillé	nous	avions	travaillé
tu	avais	travaillé	vous	aviez	travaillé
il	avait	travaillé	ils	avaient	travaillé
elle	avait	travaillé	elles	avaient	travaillé
on	avait	travaillé			

Use

Hier, j'ai vu un oiseau que je n'**avais** jamais **vu** avant.
J'étais content quand le travail **était fini**.

The pluperfect describes events that occurred before another event in the past.

The pluperfect frequently is introduced by **quand** or **après que**.

Quand elle **était rentrée** de son travail, elle préparait le dîner.

In connection with a main clause in the imperfect, the pluperfect is used for repeated events in the past.

Si j'**avais voulu**, j'aurais terminé le travail.

If a condition no longer can be fulfilled, the pluperfect is always used in the **si** clause.

▸ On **si** clauses, see the section starting on p. 131

Pluperfect

1. Using the following infinitives, form the pluperfect. *

a) avoir (je)   __j'avais eu__

b) vivre (il)   _____

c) rire (nous)   _____

d) voir (elles)   _____

e) mettre (tu)   _____

f) vouloir (je)   _____

g) aller (elle)   _____

h) prendre (ils)   _____

i) venir (elles)   _____

j) savoir (vous)   _____

k) faire (je)   _____

l) dire (vous)   _____

m) tomber (tu)   _____

n) vaincre (je)   _____

o) dormir (ils)   _____

p) vivre (elle)   _____

q) naître (il)   _____

r) recevoir (je)   _____

s) pouvoir (tu)   _____

t) tomber (ils)   _____

u) arriver (elle)   _____

v) être (elles)   _____

w) avoir (je)   _____

x) rester (elle)   _____

2. Fill in the blanks with the pluperfect. *

la veille – *eve*
(day before)

a) Mon amie __était partie__ la veille. (partir)

b) Elle _____ la voiture. (prendre)

c) Elle _____ une lettre de son patron. (recevoir)

d) Il l' _____ dehors. (jeter)

3. Fill in the blanks with the appropriate forms of the compound past, imperfect, or pluperfect. ***

a) Dimanche dernier, nous __avons pris__ le train pour rentrer des vacances (prendre).

b) Dans le train, nous _____ la connaissance d'un couple suisse. (faire).

c) Nous _____ épuisés et fatigués mais ils nous _____ tous les détails (être / raconter).

d) Ils _____ leurs vacances en Italie (passer).

e) D'abord, ils _____ la capitale (visiter).

f) Le Colisée et les musées vaticans les _____ le plus (impressionner).

g) Puis, ils _____ à Venise (aller).

h) Là, ils _____ une promenade en gondole (faire).

i) Quand le gondolier _____, ils _____ peur (tourner / avoir).

j) L'après-midi, ils _____ pour Vérone (partir).

k) Aux arènes, ils _____ à l'opéra Aida (assister).

l) Pendant tout le voyage en train, ils _____ de nous expliquer les détails (ne pas arrêter).

m) Puis, nous _____ au revoir et nous nous _____ dans un autre compartiment (dire / installer).

n) Là, nous _____ le calme (trouver).

o) Mais les Suisses nous _____ et les explications _____ (retrouver / continuer).

Simple Past

① Le jour **fut**.

② Les animaux **eurent** soif.

③ Puis, il **firent** du bruit.

1. Day broke. 2. The animals got hungry. 3. Then they made noise.

You don't need an active mastery of the simple past tense forms. It is sufficient to recognize them when you read them.

Endings of the Simple Past

	Verbs ending in **–er**	Verbs ending in **–ir**	Verbs ending in **–dre**
je	regard**ai**	fin**is**	rend**is**
tu	regard**as**	fin**is**	rend**is**
il / elle / on	regard**a**	fin**it**	rend**it**
nous	regard**âmes**	fin**îmes**	rend**îmes**
vous	regard**âtes**	fin**îtes**	rend**îtes**
ils / elles	regard**èrent**	fin**irent**	rend**irent**

The most frequently used forms of the simple past are the third person singular and the third person plural.

Important irregular forms in the third person

être	**il fut**	**ils furent**
avoir	**il eut**	**ils eurent**
boire	**il but**	**ils burent**
croire	**il crut**	**ils crurent**
devoir	**il dut**	**ils durent**
dire	**il dit**	**ils dirent**
écrire	**il écrivit**	**ils écrivirent**
faire	**il fit**	**ils furent**
lire	**il lut**	**ils lurent**
mettre	**il mit**	**ils mirent**
pouvoir	**il put**	**ils purent**
rire	**il rit**	**ils rirent**

savoir	**il sut**	**ils surent**
venir	**il vint**	**ils vinrent**
voir	**il vit**	**ils virent**
vouloir	**il voulut**	**ils voulurent**

Use

The simple past is almost exclusively a literary phenomenon. It is found in narrative and historical texts. The most commonly occurring forms are the third person singular and the third person plural. Otherwise, the simple past performs the same function as the compound past.

In journalistic writing, one occasionally finds the simple past forms of avoir (**"il eut / ils eurent"**) and être (**"il fut / ils furent"**).

Practice and Application

1. Replace the simple past forms below with the compound past. **

a) Ce jour-là, un cheval **sortit** de l'étable.

Ce jour-là, un cheval __est sorti__ de l'étable.

b) Il **but** de l'eau dans un abreuvoir.

Il _____ de l'eau dans un abreuvoir.

c) Il se **mit** à hennir et **fit** un saut.

Il _____ à hennir et _____ un saut.

d) Il **dit** bonjour à une vache, mais la vache ne lui **répondit** pas.

Il _____ bonjour à une vache, mais la vache _____.

e) Le cheval **se fâcha** et la vache **eut** peur.

Le cheval _____ et la vache _____ peur.

f) Puis ils **lurent** sur un panneau : « Il est interdit de parler. »

Puis ils _____ sur un panneau : « Il est interdit de parler. »

g) Les deux se **regardèrent** et **rirent**.

Les deux _____ et _____.

h) À partir de ce moment-là, ils **surent** qu'il y avait des hommes.

À partir de ce moment-là, ils _____ qu'il y a des hommes.

i) Puis, les deux **s'en allèrent** et **s'installèrent** dans un pré lointain.

Puis, les deux _____ et _____ dans un pré lointain.

j) Un jour, un homme **vint** et **vit** les deux animaux dans le pré.

Un homme _____ et _____ les deux animaux dans le pré.

k) Il **voulut** savoir pourquoi les deux animaux étaient devenus des amis.

Il _____ savoir pourquoi les deux animaux étaient devenus des amis.

▶ On the use of the
compound past
and the interaction
between the
compound past
and imperfect, see
p. 87 and p. 93

l'abreuvoir – *watering trough*
broyer – *to crush, grind*

fâché – *angry*

Simple Future

1. Dans quinze jours, je partirai pour l'Espagne.

2. Je me reposerai au soleil.

---

1. In two weeks I will leave for Spain. 2. I'm going there to take a rest.

Formation

1. Endings

The endings of the simple future are regular for all verbs.

Je cherche**rai**	nous cherche**rons**
tu cherche**ras**	vous cherche**rez**
il cherche**ra**	ils cherche**ront**
elle cherche**ra**	elles cherche**ront**
on cherche**ra**	

2. Derivations

– regular derivation for verbs ending in **-er**:

The majority of the verb groups ending in **-er** form the simple future by attaching the appropriate personal endings of the simple future to the first person singular of the present tense.

j'achète	▶ j'achète**rai**	je jette	▶ je jette**rai**
j'aime	▶ j'aime**rai**	je mange	▶ je mange**rai**
j'appelle	▶ j'appelle**rai**	je nettoie	▶ je nettoie**rai**
j'appuie	▶ j'appuie**rai**	je paie	▶ je paie**rai**
j'épelle	▶ je épelle**rai**	je pèse	▶ je pèse**rai**
j'essaie	▶ j'essaie**rai**	je place	▶ je place**rai**
je change	▶ je change**rai**	je prononce	▶ je prononce**rai**
je commence	▶ je commence**rai**		

– irregular derivation for verbs ending in **-er**:

For verbs of the group **é(...)er**, attach the appropriate personal endings for the simple future to the infinitive stem, that is, to the infinitive minus **-r-** (espére-rai).

assiéger	▶ j'assiége**rai**	exagérer	▶ j'exagére**rai**
céder	▶ je céde**rai**	posséder	▶ je posséde**rai**
compléter	▶ je compléte**rai**	préférer	▶ je préfére**rai**
espérer	▶ j'espére**rai**	répéter	▶ je répéte**rai**

The verbs **aller** and **envoyer** have irregular future stems.

> **Note these two exceptions!**

aller	▶ j'i**rai**
envoyer	▶ j'enver**rai**

– regular derivation for verbs ending in **-ir** and **-re**:

For most verb groups ending in **-ir** and **-re**, attach the appropriate personal endings of the simple future to the infinitive stem (fini-rai, rend-rai).

atteindre	▶ j'atteind**rai**	lire	▶ je li**rai**
battre	▶ je batt**rai**	mettre	▶ je mett**rai**
boire	▶ je boi**rai**	naître	▶ je naît**rai**
bouillir	▶ je bouilli**rai**	offrir	▶ j'offri**rai**
choisir	▶ je choisi**rai**	ouvrir	▶ j'ouvri**rai**
conclure	▶ je conclu**rai**	peindre	▶ je peind**rai**
connaître	▶ je connaît**rai**	plaindre	▶ je plaind**rai**
construire	▶ je construi**rai**	plaire	▶ je plai**rai**
coudre	▶ je coud**rai**	prendre	▶ je prend**rai**
couvrir	▶ je couvri**rai**	ralentir	▶ je ralenti**rai**
craindre	▶ je craind**rai**	rendre	▶ je rend**rai**
croire	▶ je croi**rai**	réussir	▶ je réussi**rai**
dire	▶ je di**rai**	rire	▶ je ri**rai**
dormir	▶ je dormi**rai**	sentir	▶ je senti**rai**
écrire	▶ j'écri**rai**	servir	▶ je servi**rai**
finir	▶ je fini**rai**	sortir	▶ je sorti**rai**
fuir	▶ je fui**rai**	suivre	▶ je suiv**rai**
joindre	▶ je joind**rai**	traduire	▶ je tradui**rai**
		vivre	▶ je viv**rai**

– irregular future stems:

acquérir	▶ j'acquer**rai**	falloir	▶ il faud**ra**
aller	▶ j'i**rai**	mourir	▶ je mour**rai**
apercevoir	▶ j'apercev**rai**	mouvoir	▶ je mouv**rai**
asseoir	▶ j'assié**rai**	pleuvoir	▶ il pleuv**ra**
avoir	▶ j'au**rai**	pouvoir	▶ je pour**rai**
conquérir	▶ je conquer**rai**	recevoir	▶ je recev**rai**
courir	▶ je cour**rai**	savoir	▶ je sau**rai**
décevoir	▶ je décev**rai**	se souvenir	▶ je me souvien**drai**
devenir	▶ je devien**drai**	tenir	▶ je tien**drai**
devoir	▶ je dev**rai**	valoir	▶ il vau**drai**
envoyer	▶ j'enver**rai**	venir	▶ je vien**drai**
être	▶ je se**rai**	voir	▶ je ver**rai**
faire	▶ je fe**rai**	vouloir	▶ je vou**drai**

Use

Je vous **rendrai** votre argent la semaine prochaine.
Votre mari **sera** un avocat réputé.

▌ The simple future describes future events. It is generally the same as in English. Usually the French simple future may be expressed in English with the present progressive.
"I'll give your money back to you next week." –
"I'm going to give your money back to you next week."

▶ On the use of the present tense to express the future, see p. 72

Nous espérons que vous **trouverez** notre hôtel facilement.

▌ After expressions that point to the future, such as espérer, French commonly uses the simple future.

Si tu vas en Bretagne l'année prochaine, tu **diras** bonjour à madame Legrand.

▌ If the condition of a **si** clause can be fulfilled, the main clause uses either the present or the simple future.

▶ On **si** clauses, see the section starting on p. 131

Near Future

Demain, je vais ache-
ter une voiture.

①

Tu ne vas pas dépenser
tout notre argent ?

②

1. Tomorrow I'm going to buy a car. 2. You're not going to spend all our money, are you?

Formation

The near future, or **futur composé**, is formed with the present tense
of the verb **aller** and an appropriate infinitive.

je	**vais**	**partir**	nous	**allons**	**partir**
tu	**vas**	**partir**	vous	**allez**	**partir**
il/elle/on	**va**	**partir**	ils/elles	**vont**	**partir**

Use

Qu'est-ce que tu **vas faire** à Paris ? – Je **vais** me **promener** toute la
journée.

The near future describes events in the future. Usually it can be
replaced with a form of the simple future.

Simple Future and Near Future

J'espère qu'il ne **va** pas **pleuvoir**.
Demain, il ne **pleuvra** pas.

The near future is more commonly used in spoken French; the simple future is used in both literary and colloquial French.

Qu'est-ce qu'on **va faire** maintenant ?
– Je **vais** vous **préparer** un bon repas.

The near future refers to something that is just about to happen (in connection with **maintenant** or **tout de suite**) or expresses an intention.

English sometimes uses present forms with future meaning, with an appropriate adverb: "I'm doing it tomorrow." French rarely uses the present for future events.

▶ On the use of the present, see p. 72

Simple Future and Near Future

1. Olivier, a teenager, is thinking about his future. What will things be like in a few years?
Change the text by replacing the present tense forms with the corresponding forms of the simple future. *

a) Je _ferai___ mes études à l'université de Toulouse. (faire)

b) Je _____ médecin. (devenir)

c) J'_____ une femme. (avoir)

d) Ma femme et moi, nous _____ des enfants. (avoir)

e) Je _____ dans un hôpital. (travailler)

f) Nous _____ tous les deux de nos enfants. (s'occuper)

g) Nous _____ une maison à la campagne.

(faire construire)

h) Nos enfants _____ dans la cour. (jouer)

i) Je _____ mes grands-parents tous les dimanches. (voir)

j) Je _____ beaucoup d'argent. (posséder)

k) En été, nous _____ en vacances sur la côte d'Azur. (aller)

l) Je _____ du sport et j' _____ à faire de la planche à voile.

(pratiquer / apprendre)

m) Il ne _____ pas et sur la plage, on _____ pendant des

heures. (pleuvoir / lire)

n) Le soir, on _____ le dîner dans un petit restaurant. (prendre)

o) Nous _____ des cartes postales à nos amis. (envoyer)

2. Rewrite these sentences, replacing the simple future with the near future. *

a) Je commencerai à apprendre le français en avril.

  _Je vais commencer à apprendre le français en avril._____

b) Tu diras bonjour à ta mère.

  _____

c) A partir de demain, tu ne boiras plus.

  _____

d) A la montagne, nous dormirons bien.

_____

e) Vous reviendrez l'année prochaine ?

_____

f) Demain soir, on parlera du nouveau film.

_____

g) Est-ce que nous ferons du ski pendant les vacances ?

_____

h) J'espère qu'il ne pleuvra pas demain.

_____

i) Ma fille sera une grande actrice.

_____

j) Vous regarderez un film samedi prochain ?

_____

3. Rewrite these sentences, using the simple future and the negation
ne ... plus. ******

a) L'année dernière, nous avons passé nos vacances dans les Alpes.

  Mais nous ne passerons plus nos vacances dans les Alpes.

b) On allait à Chamonix depuis dix ans.

  _____

c) On prenait toujours une chambre à l'hôtel.

  _____

d) Cette fois-ci, nous avons dormi dans une petite chambre.

  _____

e) Je m'ennuyais sur la piste.

s'ennuyer – *to be bored*

  _____

f) J'ai envoyé des cartes postales à nos amis. Je les ai tenu au courant.

tenir qn au courant –
*to keep someone
informed*

  _____

  _____

Simple Future and Near Future

s'installer au comptoir –
*to ensconce oneself at
the bar (counter)*

g) Tous les soirs mon mari buvait au bar. Il s'installait souvent au comptoir.

_____

_____

avoir sommeil – *to be
sleepy*

h) Moi, j'étais fatiguée. J'avais sommeil.

_____

i) Un jour, j'ai vu une photo de mon mari dans un journal.

_____

faire semblant de faire
qch – *to pretend to do
something*

j) J'ai fait semblant de ne rien voir.

_____

tromper qn – *to deceive,
betray someone*

k) Il m'avait trompé.

_____

l) Sur la photo, on voyait mon mari avec une autre femme.

_____

Future Perfect

Dès que j'**aurai passé** le bac, je partirai aux Etats-Unis. ①

② Dès que je **serai arrivé**, je te passerai un message.

1. *Once I've gotten my high school diploma, I'll go to the United States.*
2. *Once I've arrived, I'll send you an e-mail.*

Formation

The future perfect, or **futur antérieur**, is made up of the simple future of **avoir** or **être** and the past participle.

j'	aurai	préparé	nous	aurons	préparé
tu	auras	préparé	vous	aurez	préparé
il	aura	préparé	ils	auront	préparé
elle	aura	préparé	elles	auront	préparé
on	aura	préparé			

▶ On the formation and variability of the past participle and on the use of avoir or être, see the section on the compound past, starting on p. 83

Use

Il est dix heures. A midi, mon mari **aura préparé** le repas.

The future perfect is used for a future occurrence ("préparer le repas") that will have ended <u>before</u> a future point in time ("à midi").

Quand nous **aurons déjeuné**, il fera la vaisselle.

The future perfect is also used for a future event ("déjeuner") that will have been completed before another future event ("faire la vaisselle").

Practice and Application

1. The Floret family will have an exhausting day. Fill in the blanks below with the preceding verb in each case. **

faire la lessive –
to do the laundry

le sèche-linge –
clothes dryer

passer l'aspirateur –
to run the vacuum

le carrelage – *tiled floor*

faire les vitres – *to clean
the windows*

faire les courses –
*to go shopping, run
errands*

faire du footing –
to go jogging

a) Quand mon mari aura fait la vaisselle, il fera une lessive.

b) Quand il ___aura fait___ la lessive, il mettra le linge au sèche-linge.

c) Quand il _____ le linge au sèche-linge, il passera l'aspirateur.

d) Quand il _____ l'aspirateur, il repassera.

e) Quand il _____ , il nettoiera le carrelage de la cuisine.

f) Quand il _____ le carrelage de la cuisine, il fera les vitres.

g) Quand il _____ les vitres, il ira en ville pour faire les courses.

h) Quand il _____ en ville pour faire les courses, il sortira notre chien.

i) Quand il _____ notre chien, il fera un footing.

j) Quand il _____ fait un footing, il se promènera avec les enfants.

k) Quand il _____ avec les enfants, il rentrera à la maison.

l) Quand il _____ à la maison, il se mettra un peu au lit.

m) Quand il _____ un peu au lit, je reviendrai du bureau.

n) Quand je _____ du bureau, on se préparera pour sortir.

o) Quand on _____ pour sortir, on ira au cinéma.

p) Quand on _____ au cinéma, on dansera dans une boîte.

q) Quand on _____ dans une boîte, on prendra un petit repas.

r) Quand on _____ un petit repas, on retrera chez nous.

s) Quand on _____ chez nous, on se couchera.

t) Quand on _____ , on se réveillera pour une nouvelle journée bien fatigante.

112

Present Conditional

« Nous aimerions venir, mais mon mari est en voyage d'affaires. Il m'a dit qu'il reviendrait demain. »

①

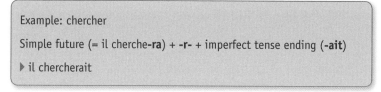

1. We would love to come, but my husband is on a business trip. He told me he would be back tomorrow.

Formation

1. Endings

j'	aime**rais**	nous	aime**rions**
tu	aime**rais**	vous	aime**riez**
il	aime**rait**	ils	aime**raient**
elle	aime**rait**	elles	aime**raient**
on	aime**rait**		

> For the present conditional, the same rules of derivation apply as for the simple future (see p. 103)

The endings of the present conditional are the same for all verbs. They are composed of an **-r-** and the endings of the imperfect tense.

2. Derivations

Derivations as for the simple future + **-r-** + imperfect tense ending

> Example: chercher
>
> Simple future (= il cherche-**ra**) + **-r-** + imperfect tense ending (**-ait**)
>
> ▶ il chercherait

113

Present Conditional

Use

le lendemain –
the following day

Elle m'a annoncé qu'elle **partirait** le lendemain.
Je pensais qu'elle se **présenterait** devant le jury d'examen.

▎The conditional is used as the "future of the past" for events that, viewed from the past, take place at a later time.

Pourriez-vous me montrer le chemin ?
Je vous **serais** reconnaissant de bien vouloir confirmer la réservation.
Je **voudrais** vous demander si vous pouvez me prêter de l'argent.

▎The conditional is used to express a polite request or a wish …

Je **pourrais** faire un voyage autour du monde. Mais je n'ai pas assez d'argent.
Ne parlez pas. L'enfant s'**éveillerait**.

s'éveiller – *to wake up, waken*

▎– or to express a possibility or an assumption.

Moi, je **serais** le roi et toi, tu **serais** la reine.

▎Children use the conditional to assign roles.

le taux de chômage –
unemployment rate
augmenter – *to increase*

Le taux de chômage **augmenterait** à quinze pour cent.

▎In journalistic writing, the conditional is used to express assumptions with caution.

Si je gagnais au loto, je **ferais** un voyage autour du monde.

▶ On **si** clauses, see the section starting on p. 131

▎After the imperfect in a **si** clause, the conditional is used in the main clause.

Au cas où nous **serions** absents quand vous viendrez, la clé est sous le paillasson.

le paillasson – *mat, doormat*

▎After the following expressions, which set a condition, the conditional is used: **au cas où**, **dans le cas où**, **pour le cas où**, **dans l'hypothèse où**.

Past Conditional

① Selon notre correspondant, des manifestants auraient endommagé des voitures.

② Ils auraient aussi cassé des vitrines de grands magasins.

---

1. *According to our correspondent, some demonstrators have damaged cars.*
2. *They also are said to have broken display windows of department stores.*

Formation

The past conditional (conditional perfect) is made up of the present conditional of **avoir** or **être** and the past participle.

j'	aurais	réussi		nous	aurions	réussi
tu	aurais	réussi		vous	auriez	réussi
il	aurait	réussi		ils	auraient	réussi
elle	aurait	réussi		elles	auraient	réussi
on	aurait	réussi				

▶ On the formation and variability of the past participle and on the use of **avoir** or **être**, see the section on the compound past, starting on p. 83

Use

Le ministre des Affaires Etrangères **aurait démissionné.**
Un groupe de jeunes **aurait tué** un étranger.

■ In journalistic writing, the past conditional is used to be cautious in describing events that have happened but are not yet officially confirmed (English "allegedly").

Si tu avais travaillé, tu **aurais passé** ton bac.

■ After a pluperfect verb in the **si** clause, the past conditional is used in the main clause.

démissionner – *to quit, resign*

passer le bac – *to receive one's high school diploma*

▶ On **si** clauses, see the section starting on p. 131

Conditional

1. Form the present conditional of the following infinitives. *

a) payer (je)   <u>je payerais oder je paierais</u>

b) mettre (elles)   _____

c) faire (on)   _____

d) vouloir (ils)   _____

e) devoir (tu)   _____

f) voir (il)   _____

g) vouloir (nous)   _____

h) dire (elle)   _____

i) aller (je)   _____

j) être (vous)   _____

k) manger (tu)   _____

l) suivre (ils)   _____

m) vivre (on)   _____

o) tenir (je)   _____

2. Newspaper articles often are cautious in their reporting. Write sentences in the past conditional. *

a) Ils – tuer – des étrangers

<u>Ils auraient tué des étrangers.</u>

b) Le président – mentir.

_____

c) Le premier ministre – démissionner

_____

d) Des rebelles – prendre le pouvoir

_____

e) Le parlement – être en flamme

_____

3. Fill in the blanks below with the appropriate forms of the present conditional. Be sure to express yourself very politely. **

M. = Monsieur;
Mme. = Madame

a) M. _Pourriez-vous_ m'expliquer le chemin pour aller à Versailles?

b) Mme. Je _____ bien mais je_____ prendre tout de suite le bus.

c) M. _____ la gentillesse de m'indiquer au moins la direction ?

d) Mme. Je _____ vous indiquer la direction, mais ne le fais par car je _____ le bus.

~~Pouvoir~~

aimer

avoir

vouloir

povoir

rater

4. Translate these sentences, using the present conditional or the past conditional. ***

a) Could you help me?

  Pourriez-vous m'aider ?

b) I would like to ask you whether you could lend me some money.

  _____

c) We could go to the movies this evening.

  _____

d) Ask him whether he would agree.

  _____

e) He asked me whether someone would come.

  _____

f) Foreign troops are said to have murdered the president.

  _____

des troupes étrangères –
foreign troops

g) In case they come, you fix breakfast.

  _____

h) I should have learned a different occupation.

  _____

i) The German ambassador is said to have died.

  _____

l'ambassadeur
allemand – *the
German ambassador*

j) I could eat an enormous (serving of) ice cream.

  _____

Present Subjunctive

Il faut que tu ailles au supermarché pour que je puisse nous préparer un repas. ①

---

1. You have to go [It is necessary that you go] to the supermarket so I can fix a meal for us.

Formation

1. Endings

Il faut que je	sort**e**.	Il faut que nous	sort**ions**.
Il faut que tu	sort**es**.	Il faut que vous	sort**iez**.
Il faut qu'il	sort**e**.	Il faut qu'ils	sort**ent**.
Il faut qu'elle	sort**e**.	Il faut qu'elles	sort**ent**.
Il faut qu'on	sort**e**.		

The endings of the subjunctive are regular. There are only two exceptions: **avoir** and **être**.

avoir	**être**
que j'aie	que je soi**s**
que tu aies	que tu soi**s**
qu'il ai**t**	qu'il soit
que nous a**y**ons	que nous so**y**ons
que vous a**y**ez	que vous so**y**ez
qu'ils aient	qu'ils soient

2. Derivations

Regular derivation:

> Stem of the third person plural present tense + subjunctive ending

Most regular and irregular verbs form the subjunctive in this way: Take the stem of the third person plural present tense, and add the appropriate personal endings (que je **batt-e**).

ils aiment	▸ que j'aim**e**	ils mettent	▸ que je mett**e**
ils s'assoient	▸ que je m'assoi**e**	ils naissent	▸ que je naiss**e**
ils battent	▸ que je batt**e**	ils ouvrent	▸ que j'ouvr**e**
ils concluent	▸ que je conclu**e**	ils plaisent	▸ que je plais**e**
ils conduisent	▸ que je conduis**e**	ils prennent	▸ que je prenn**e**
ils connaissent	▸ que je connaiss**e**	ils rendent	▸ que je rend**e**
ils courent	▸ que je cour**e**	ils résolvent	▸ que je résolv**e**
ils craignent	▸ que je craign**e**	ils rient	▸ que je ri**e**
ils disent	▸ que je dis**e**	ils servent	▸ que je serv**e**
ils dorment	▸ que je dorm**e**	ils suivent	▸ que je suiv**e**
ils écrivent	▸ que j'écriv**e**	ils se taisent	▸ que je me tais**e**
ils finissent	▸ que je finiss**e**	ils vainquent	▸ que je vainqu**e**
ils lisent	▸ que je lis**e**	ils vivent	▸ que je viv**e**
ils mentent	▸ que je ment**e**		

Regular derivations with a change in the stem vowel:

Verbs that change in the stem vowel in the present tense retain this change in the subjunctive.

- verbs ending in **-er**, such as **peser: je pèse**, but: **nous pesions**;

que je pèse	que nous pesions	Also: jeter, appeler, acheter, peler, espérer
que tu pèses	que vous pesiez	
qu'il pèse	qu'ils pèsent	

- irregular verbs: **je bois**, but: **nous buvions**.

que je boive	que nous buvions	Also: acquérir, devoir, mourir, mouvoir, prendre, recevoir, tenir, venir
que tu boives	que vous buviez	
qu'il boive	qu'ils boivent	

Regular derivation for verbs with a **-y-** before forms stressed on the ending (first and second person plural):

Verbs that exhibit a **-y-** before present tense forms stressed on the ending retain this **-y-** in the subjunctive as well.

que je nettoie	que nous nettoyions	Also: appuyer, payer, envoyer
que tu nettoies	que vous nettoyiez	
qu'il nettoie	qu'ils nettoient	

que je voie	que nous voyions	Also: croire, se distraire
que tu voies	que vous voyiez	
qu'il voie	qu'ils voient	

Irregular subjunctive stems:

avoir	que j'a**ie** qu'il ai**t** que nous **a**yons
être	que je **sois** que tu **sois** qu'il **soit** que nous **soyons**
aller	que j'**aille** que nous **allions**
faire	que je **fasse** que nous **fassions**
falloir	qu'il **faille**
pleuvoir	qu'il **pleuve**
pouvoir	que je **puisse** que nous **puissions**
savoir	que je **sache** que nous **sachions**
valoir	que je **vaille** que nous **valions**
vouloir	que je **veuille** que nous **voulions**

Past Subjunctive

1. Let's assume that he lied. 2. I want him to be punished.

Formation

The past subjunctive is made up of the subjunctive of **avoir** or **être** and the past participle.

Admettons	que j'	**aie dit**	la vérité.
	que tu	**aies dit**	
	qu'il / elle	**ait dit**	
	que nous	**ayons dit**	
	que vous	**ayez dit**	
	qu'ils / elles	**aient dit**	
Il souhaite	que je	**sois**	puni(e).
	que tu	**sois**	puni (e).
	qu'il / elle	**soit**	puni (e).
	que nous	**soyons**	puni(e)s.
	que vous	**soyez**	puni(e) (s).
	qu'ils / elles	**soient**	puni(e) (s).

▶ On the formation and variability of the past participle and on the use of **avoir** or **être**, see the section on the compound past, starting on p. 83

Use of the Present Subjunctive and Past Subjunctive

The subjunctive occurs almost exclusively in subordinate clauses after **que**.

Two types of usage are distinguished: main (principal) clauses that automatically trigger the subjunctive following **que**, and main clauses in which there is an option (such as subjunctive or present tense).

Some verbs, expressions, and conjunctions absolutely require the subjunctive. It is advisable to memorize them as you learn them!

1. Obligatory Use of the Subjunctive

After verbs expressing desirability or insistence:

> Je **veux qu'**il **apprenne** le français.
> **Permettez que** je vous **dise** la vérité.
> J'**interdis que** vous **pénétriez** dans mon terrain.
> Je n'**accepte** pas **que** mes enfants **fassent** ce devoir.

> préférer que, demander que, proposer que, refuser que, vouloir bien que, aimer mieux que, désirer que, souhaiter que, aimer que, avoir envie que, exiger que, ordonner que, autoriser que, défendre que

After verbs and expressions of emotion:

> Elle **apprécie que** les Français **achètent** souvent chez les petits commerçants.
> Nous **regrettons que** vous **ayez perdu** votre travail.
> J'**aimerais que** tu **sortes** avec ce garçon.
> Je **trouve important que** les ouvriers **fassent** la grève.
> Je **suis triste qu'**elle **soit** partie.

> détester que, adorer que, admirer que, avoir honte que, avoir peur que, craindre que, critiquer que, déplorer que, s'étonner que, s'inquiéter que, se moquer que, trouver bien / mal / important que, être heureux / satis-fait / étonné / désolé / fâché / fier / ravi / content / surpris

After impersonal verbs and expressions:

> **Il faut que** tu **fasses** la vaisselle.
> **Il vaut mieux que** tu t'en **ailles**.
> **C'est une honte qu'**on **jette** de la nourriture.
> **C'est bizarre qu'**il n'**ait** pas **répondu**.
> **C'est dommage** qu'on ne **soit** pas là.

une honte – *shame, disgrace*

> il est normal / nécessaire / bon / mauvais / possible / intéressant / faux / honteux / triste / juste / injuste / naturel / utile / inutile / étrange / indis-pensable / surprenant que, c'est bien / mal / malheureux / drôle / sen-sationnel / rare / terrible / nécessaire que

After a number of conjunctions:

> **Bien qu'**elle **aille** mieux maintenant, la situation reste difficile.
> L'Etat dépense plus d'argent **pour que** l'économie **reprenne**.
> J'aimerais voir encore une fois ton bébé **avant que** vous vous en **alliez**.

▶ On conjunctions, see the section starting on p. 201

> quoique, sans que, malgré que, jusqu'à ce que, en attendant que, afin que, à condition que, pourvu que, à supposer que, à moins que

The subjunctive also is found in certain fixed expressions:

Dieu **soit** loué!	*Thank God!*
Vive la France!	*Long live France!*

2. Optional Use of the Subjunctive

If verbs and expressions of thinking and giving opinions are negated, **que** usually is followed by the subjunctive.

> Crois-tu qu'il fera beau demain ? –
> Non, je **ne crois pas qu'**il **fasse** beau demain.
> Tu trouves qu'il est méchant ? –
> Non, je **ne trouve pas qu'**il **soit** méchant.

> ne pas penser que, ne pas être sur que, ne pas espérer que, ne pas être certain que

After **supposer** and **admettre**, depending on the meaning, either the subjunctive or the present can be used:

	Meaning in Present	Meaning in Subjunctive
supposer:	*to imagine*	*to presume*
admettre:	*to admit*	*to assume*

> Je suppose que vous avez l'intention de nous aider.
> Je **suppose que** vous **ayez** l'intention de nous aider.

After verbs of saying, telling, and explaining, the subjunctive appears if they are used in the sense of giving instructions to someone ("should, ought").

> crier, faire savoir, téléphoner

J'ai écrit qu'il est imprudent.	Je lui **ai écrit qu'**il **soit** prudent.
Dis-lui que je l'attends.	**Dis-lui** qu'il m'**attende**.

▶ On relative clauses, see p. 63

In a relative clause, the subjunctive is used if a wish is expressed. If a fact is being stated, however, the present is used.

Je cherche un Français qui **sache** parler le japonais.
Je connais un Français qui sait parler le japonais.

▶ On the comparative, see p. 168

Superlatives often can be substantiated only by <u>subjective evaluations</u> or <u>assessments</u>. In such cases, the following relative clause contains the subjunctive. If a <u>fact</u> is being stated, however, the present is used.

Madeleine est la femme **la plus** charmante que je **connaisse**.
L'orange est **le seul** fruit qui **soit** bon.
C'est le premier homme qui a mis le pied sur la lune.

Present Subjunctive or Past Subjunctive?

The present subjunctive is used when the action of the **que** clause occurs <u>during</u> or <u>after</u> the action of the main clause.

J'ai peur qu'elle **parte** <u>aujourd'hui</u>.
J'ai peur qu'elle **parte** <u>demain</u>.

J'avais peur qu'elle **parte** <u>ce jour-là</u>.
J'avais peur qu'elle **parte** <u>le lendemain</u>.

But the past subjunctive is used when the action of the **que** clause occurs <u>before</u> the action of the main clause.

J'ai peur qu'elle **soit partie** <u>hier</u>.
J'avais peur qu'elle **soit partie** <u>la veille</u>.

The English subjunctive cannot be equated with the French subjunctive. English tends to avoid or omit the subjunctive; in French, it is in common use.

1. Using the words supplied below, form subjunctives. *

a) lire (je)   _que je lise_

b) dormir (il)   _____

c) pouvoir (elle)   _____

d) pleuvoir (il)   _____

e) aller (je)   _____

f) être (nous)   _____

g) finir (vous)   _____

h) prendre (tu)   _____

i) savoir (ils)   _____

j) écrire (je)   _____

k) vouloir (elles)   _____

l) avoir (je)   _____

m) boire (nous)   _____

n) prendre (vous)   _____

2. Complete the sentences below with the appropriate form of the subjunctive mood. **

a) Il ne veut pas apprendre le français.

Je veux qu' _il apprenne le français_ .

b) Elle n'est pas partie.

Je souhaite qu' _____ .

c) Il ne travaille pas.

J'exige que _____ .

d) L'enfant n'est pas sage.

J'aimerais qu' _____ .

e) Elle lit beaucoup au lit.

Je n'aime pas qu' _____ .

f) La phrase n'est pas correcte.

Je demande qu' _____ .

Subjunctive

g) Il ne pleure plus depuis deux heures.

C'est surprenant qu' _____ .

h) Elle ne sait pas compter.

Il est indispensable qu' _____ .

i) Il veut un téléviseur.

Il est normal qu'il _____ .

j) Elle va en vacances.

Il est nécessaire qu' _____ .

k) Tu n'achètes plus de viande.

Je trouve bien que _____ .

l) Elle ne me tient plus au courant.

Je suis fâché qu' _____ .

m) Il ne boit plus.

Je suis surprise qu' _____ .

n) Tu es contente.

Je ne crois pas que _____ .

3. Decide whether the subjunctive is needed. ***

a) J'espère que vous ___allez___ bien. (aller)

b) Il dit que vous _____ une faute. (avoir fait)

c) Il est indispensable que tu _____ la leçon. (apprendre)

d) C'est dommage que votre maison n'_____ pas une pièce
de plus. (avoir)

e) Je crois que M. Dutour _____ en vacances. (être parti)

f) Nous trouvons bien que vous _____ vos vacances en
Suisse. (passer)

g) Je connais un cinéma qui _____ des réductions aux
étudiants tous les soirs. (faire)

h) Ce sont les plus belles vacances que nous _____ .
(avoir passé)

i)   Faut-il que j'_____ chercher un médecin? (aller)

j)   Je veux que tu _____ aux examens. (réussir)

4.   Why is the subjunctive used in the following sentences? Match the French sentences with the correct statements below. ***

_____   1.   Je veux que tu saches la vérité.

_____   2.   Je cherche une nouvelle voiture qui ne soit pas trop chère.

_____   3.   Il trouve bien qu'on ait décidé une monnaie unique.

_____   4.   Il est injuste que les salariés paient tellement d'impôts.

_____   5.   Nous restons au café de Paris jusqu'à ce que notre amie

        revienne.

_____   6.   Il faut rentrer avant qu'il fasse nuit.

_____   7.   Je ne crois pas qu'elle ait des chances de réussir.

_____   8.   Elle a dit que tu viennes.

_____   9.   Notre voiture est la plus belle qu'il y ait en ville.

a)   after an impersonal verb (obligatory use)

b)   after a verb of saying, telling, or explaining (nonobligatory use)

c)   after a superlative (nonobligatory use)

d)   after a verb expressing desirability or insistence (obligatory use)

e)   in a relative clause (nonobligatory use)

f)   after an expression of thinking and giving an opinion (nonobligatory use)

g)   after a conjunction (obligatory use)

h)   after a conjunction (obligatory use)

i)   after a verb expressing emotion (obligatory use)

Imperative

No exclamation mark is required with the French imperative.

---

1. Sit down, please. 2. Olivier, close the door. 3. Let's talk about the French Resistance.

Formation

Regular formation:

For every verb, there are three imperative forms. These forms are derived from the present tense of the:

1st Person Singular (**j'ouvre**):	**Ouvre** la fenêtre, s'il te plaît. **Attends** encore un peu pour répondre.
2nd Person Plural (**vous parlez**):	Ne **parlez** pas si fort. **Lisez** bien les informations.
1st Person Plural (**nous restons**):	**Restons** sur ce sujet. **Essayons** de continuer.

With verbs ending in **-er**, an **-s** is attached to the imperative before **"y"** and **"en"**:

| penser | ▶ Pense**s**-y. |
| aller | ▶ Va**s**-y. |

Irregular formation:

The imperative of the verbs **avoir**, **être**, and **savoir** is irregular:

avoir: **aie**, **ayons**, **ayez**	N'**ayez** pas peur.
être: **sois**, **soyons**, **soyez**	Olivier, **sois** sage.
savoir: **sache**, **sachons**, **sachez**,	**Sachez** que Paris a été libérée entre le 18 et 25 août 1944.

Use

Sortez d'ici

The imperative is used to express
– an order or a demand.

Ne réponds pas à cette question.

– a piece of advice.

Ferme les yeux et dors bien.

– a request or a wish.

Donnez-moi encore une réponse.

– or an encouragement.

> **!** With the affirmative imperative, "moi" and "toi" take the place of "me" and "te."

▶ On the placement of object pronouns, see p. 49

With the affirmative imperative, the object pronouns are appended to the verb with a hyphen (**"Asseyez-vous."**).
With the negative imperative, the object pronouns are placed, as usual, before the verb (**"Ne vous asseyez pas."**).

Replacement of the Imperative with Other Constructions

These can take the place of the imperative:

– an interrogative sentence with vouloir:
   Veux-tu sortir d'ici ?

– or pouvoir + infinitive:
   Vous pouvez me donner encore une réponse ?

– a declarative sentence with the near future:
   Vous allez rentrer tout de suite.

– or an interrogative sentence with s'il te / vous plaît.
   Tu fermes la porte, s'il te plaît ?

Imperative

1. Rewrite the following sentences, using the imperative. *

a) Je veux que tu sortes. _____Sors._____

b) Veux-tu me donner encore une réponse ? _____

c) Tu peux me passer l'éponge, s'il te plaît ? _____

d) Tu fermes la fenêtre, s'il te plaît ? _____

e) Voulez-vous lire un texte ? _____

f) Pouvez-vous me répondre ? _____

g) Vous allez sortir tout de suite vos livres. _____

h) Michel, tu sors ton livre ? _____

i) Veux-tu commencer à lire ? _____

j) Vous allez me donner la réponse tout de suite. _____

k) Voulez-vous être de bons élèves ? _____

2. Negate the following imperatives. Replace the words in **bold** with appropriate pronouns. **

a) Mes élèves, calmez-vous. _Ne vous calmez pas._

b) Asseyez-vous. _____

c) Lève-toi, Michel. _____

d) Commence à lire **le texte**. _____

e) Nettoie **le tableau**, Susanne. _____

f) Vas-y. _____

g) Complète **la phrase**, Sandra. _____

h) Dis-moi **la réponse**. _____

i) Donnez-moi **vos devoirs**. _____

j) Pensons **à l'année prochaine**. _____

y aller – *to go there*
s'en aller – *to go away, leave*

Si Clause (Conditional Clause)

1. Si je gagnais au loto, je ferais un voyage autour du monde.

---

1. If I won the lottery, I would take a trip around the world.

There are three types of **si** clauses.

1. Clauses that express a possibility with regard to the present or the future. In these cases, the condition is completely fulfillable.

Si Clause	Main Clause
Si vous **êtes** d'accord, Si + present	j'**appelle** ma voisine. present
Si tu **as** le temps ce soir, Si + present	on **ira** au théâtre. future

2. Clauses that express an improbability with regard to the present or the future. The condition can only theoretically be met.

Si Clause	Main Clause
Si je **gagnais** au loto, Si + imperfect	je m'**achèterais** une voiture de sport. present conditional

131

Si *Clause*

3. Clauses that express an impossibility with regard to the past. There is no way the condition can be met because the events are already over.

Si Clause	Main Clause
Si j'**avais passé** mon bac,	j'**aurais fait** des études à l'université.
Si + pluperfect	past conditional (conditional perfect)

<u>Note</u>: A **si** clause never contains the future or the conditional.

> **!**
> A **si** clause never contains an **r** form.

The future can be used only if the **si** introduces an indirect question.

« Je me demande si mes amis **viendront**. »

Do not confuse the **si** clause with the **quand** clause. In a **quand** clause, the "quand" can be followed by the future tense.

> si = *if* (conditional)
> Quand = *when, as soon as* (temporal)

« Quand mes amis **viendront**, nous partirons en vacances ».
(= *"When / Once / As soon as ... "*).

1. You are lying on your couch and thinking about unlikely things.
Write sentences using the words provided. *

a) je – avoir – de l'argent

    Si seulement j'avais de l'argent.

b) appartement – être plus – grand

    _____

c) je – gagner – au loto

    _____

d) je – avoir – ami

    _____

e) je – travailler – moins

    _____

f) je – aller – en vacances – cette année

    _____

g) quelqu'un – me rendre visite

    _____

h) je – vivre – à Paris

    _____

2. Fill in the blanks with the appropriate forms. **
Pay close attention to the tenses used in the individual clauses,
and follow the rules for the three possible types of **si** clauses.

a) Si vous ____ *êtes* ____ libre ce soir, on ira au restaurant. (être)

b) S'il _____ le permis de conduire, il aurait eu une voiture.

    (passer)

un permis de conduire –
driver's license

c) Si elle _____ ce soir, on ferait un tour en voiture.

    (venir)

d) Si tu m' _____ , tu me donnes un bisou. (aimer)

un bisou – *kiss*

Practice and Application

e) S'il _____ beau demain, on va déjeuner dehors. (faire)

f) Si j'avais 30 ans, je _____ un voyage autour du monde.
   (faire)

g) Si j'avais eu de l'argent, j'_____ une maison. (acheter)

h) Si j'_____ qu'il était bête, je ne me serais pas mariée
   avec lui. (savoir)

3. Translate the following sentences. Remember that a **si** clause cannot contain an **r** form. ***

a) If I had won the lottery, I would have built myself a house.

   Si j'avais gagné au loto, j'aurais construit une maison.

b) If I win the lottery, I'll buy myself a house.

   _____

c) If I won the lottery, I would buy myself a house.

   _____

d) If my boyfriend were younger, I would marry him.

   _____

e) If I had been rich, I would have bought myself a house.

   _____

Verbs with an Object

Verbs with a Direct Object

> Je veux **aider Monsieur Dutour**. Il a **besoin d'une voiture**.

1. I want to help Monsieur Dutour. He needs a car.

Direct objects are sentence complements that receive the action of a transitive verb. They are not preceded by a preposition.

> Tu **connais Catherine Deneuve** ? – Oui, je **l'ai rencontrée** l'an dernier.
> Regarde **la vieille dame** avec ses bagages. – Tu as raison. Il faut **l'**aider.

A direct object can be replaced only with a direct object pronoun (such as **le**, **la**, **les**).

Some verbs take a direct object in French, whereas their English equivalents require the use of a preposition. These include the verbs **attendre**, **chercher**, **demander**, **écouter**, **espérer**, **habiter**, **payer**, **regarder**.

> Direct objects answer the questions "Whom?" or "What?"

> Indirect objects answer the question "To or for whom?"

Verbs with an à Object

> As-tu téléphoné à ta mère ?

Have you telephoned your mother?

An **à** object often corresponds to an English indirect object.

> Elle **a cédé à Monsieur Dutour** ? – Oui, elle **lui a** cédé.
> Tu **as parlé à tes enfants** ? – Oui, mais je ne **leur parle** plus.
> Tu **as répondu à leur lettre** ? – Non, je **n'y répondrai** jamais.

In the case of persons, an **à** object usually is replaced with an indirect object pronoun (such as **lui** and **leur**); in the case of things, it is replaced with **y**.

Some verbs take an indirect object in French, whereas their English counterparts take a direct object. Some examples: **désobéir**, **échouer**, **jouer**, **plaire**, **renoncer**, **resister**, **survivre**, **téléphoner**.

> Exceptions:
> **penser** <u>à elle</u>,
> **s'intéresser** <u>à lui</u>. **!**

Verbs with an Object

Verbs with a *de* Object

> Nous rêvons d'une grande maison.

We dream of a big house.

Verbs with a **de** object are translated into English in various ways.

J'ai besoin de ma femme.
I need my wife.

– Tu **rêves** déjà **d'elle** ?
– *Are you already dreaming about her?*

Tu te souviens du Pont du Gard ?
Do you remember the pont de Gard?

– Oui, je **m'en souviens**.
– *Yes, I remember it.*

Vous **jouez de la guitare** ?
Do you play the guitar?

– Non, je n'**en joue** plus.
– *No, I don't play it anymore.*

Verbs with a Direct Object and an *à* Object

Some verbs can take both a direct object and an **à** object.

Tu **as prêté cette machine à ta fille** ?
Did you loan that machine to your daughter?

– Oui, je **la lui ai prêtée**.
– *Yes, I loaned it to her.*

Tu **as demandé de l'argent à ton fils** ?
Did you ask your son for money?

– Non, je ne **lui en ai** pas **demandé**.
– *No, I didn't ask him for any.*

> Examples: acheter, adresser, apprendre, conseiller, dire, écrire, enseigner, enlever, expliquer, interdire, montrer, présenter, promettre, raconter, rappeler, recommander, refuser, répondre, reprocher, répéter.

Verbs with a Direct Object and a *de* Object

Some verbs can take both a direct object and a **de** object.

Tu as **appris la nouvelle de ta femme** ? – Oui, je l'ai apprise **d'elle**.
Vous allez **informer votre fils de votre décision** ? – Oui, je vais **l'en informer** prochainement.

> Examples: avertir, débarrasser, équiper, prévenir, priver, remercier, obtenir, recevoir, savoir.

Reflexive Verbs

1. They are taking a walk in the park. 2. They don't talk to each other anymore.
3. She will go away soon. 4. Her firm has set up shop in Alsace.

Verbs with Reflexive and Nonreflexive Forms

Some verbs have both reflexive and nonreflexive forms.

Je vais **appeler** mon copain.
I'm going to call my friend.

Il **s'appelle** Gérard.
His name is Gérard.

Elle **baigne** son bébé.
She bathes her baby.

Je **me baigne** dans la mer.
I bathe in the sea.

Il a **levé** la main sur sa femme.
He raised his hand to his wife.

Il **s'est levé** à dix heures.
He rose at 10 o'clock.

Other examples:

appeler (*to call someone*)	s'appeler (*to be called / named*)
arrêter (*to arrest, stop someone*)	s'arrêter (*to stop, come to a halt*)
attendre (*to wait for someone*)	s'attendre à (*to expect something*)
baigner (*to bathe someone*)	se baigner (*to bathe / swim [in the sea]*)
coucher (*to put someone to bed*)	se coucher (*to go to bed*)
éteindre (*to switch something off*)	s'éteindre (*to go out, be extinguished*)
lever (*to raise, lift*)	se lever (*to rise, stand up*)
marier (*to perform a wedding*)	se marier (*to get married*)
promener (*to take someone for a walk*)	se promener (*to go for a walk*)
rappeler (*to call someone back*)	se rappeler (*to remember*)
réveiller (*to wake someone*)	se réveiller (*to awaken, wake up*)
tromper (*to deceive someone*)	se tromper (*to be mistaken*)
tuer (*to kill someone*)	se tuer (*to kill oneself*)

Verbs with Only a Reflexive Form

Les enfants **se taisent.**	*The children are quiet.*
Le prisonnier **s'est enfui**.	*The prisoner has escaped.*
Dépêche-toi.	*Hurry up.*
Tu **te souviens** encore de M. Dutour ?	*Do you still remember Monsieur Dutour?*

s'evanouir – *to faint*
se méfier de – *to mistrust, distrust*
se soucier de – *to care about something / someone*

> The following verbs occur only in reflexive form:
>
> s'en aller, s'enfuir, s'envoler, s'évanouir, se méfier de, se moquer de, se soucier de, se souvenir de, se taire.

Reflexive Verbs with Parts of the Body

To refer to doing something to parts of the body, French uses a reflexive verb with the definite article, whereas English uses a possessive:

Olivier **se lave** les mains.
Olivier washes his hands.

Nous **nous lavons** le visage tous les jours.
We wash our face every day.

Tu **te maquilles**.
You put on your makeup.

Elle **se brosse** les cheveux.
She brushes her hair.

s'amuser – *to have fun*
s'ennuyer – *to be bored*
se passer – *to happen*
se trouver – *to be (situated)*

▶ On the variability of reflexive verbs, see p. 86

▶ On reflexive pronouns, see p. 44

▶ On the placement of pronouns, see p. 49

> These verbs represent an idiomatic use of the reflexive pronoun; they do not reflect reflexive or reciprocal actions:
>
> s'amuser, se dépêcher, s'endormir, s'ennuyer, se fâcher, se passer, se reposer, se sentir, se trouver.

Impersonal Verbs and Expressions

① Il pleut depuis deux mois.

② Il paraît que le climat a changé.

③ Il faudrait que la terre soit sèche.

---

1. It has been raining for two months. 2. They say that the climate has changed.
3. The soil would have to be dry.

Examples of impersonal verbs and expressions:

> An impersonal **il** corresponds to English "it." However, this is not the only possible translation.

Il pleut. / Il neige. / Il grêle. / Il vente.
It's raining. / It's snowing. / It's hailing. / It's windy.

Il fait beau / mauvais (temps).
The weather is good / bad.

Il me faut partir bientôt.
I have to leave soon.

Il faut que je parte bientôt.
I have to leave soon.

Il ne faut pas que tu fumes.
You shouldn't smoke.

Allez les enfants, **il faut partir**.
Come on, children, we have to go.

Il faut un million d'euros pour restaurer l'église.
A million euros are needed to restore the church.

Il me faut trois escalopes.
I need three cutlets.

Il y a des gens malheureux.
There are some unhappy people.

Il me semble que les voisins sont partis en vacances.
It seems to me that the neighbors have gone on vacation.

Il paraît qu'on va doubler les impôts.
They say that taxes are going to be doubled.

Il me paraît évident que l'homme atteindra une autre planète.
It seems certain to me that man will reach another planet.

Il semble que le président ne se présentera plus aux prochaines élections.
It appears that the president will not run again in the next elections.

Il me semble que je ne vais pas réussir aux examens.
I think I'm not going to pass the exams.

Il me semble certain qu'elle a fait des fautes.
It seems certain to me that she has made mistakes.

Il me semble inutile de te convaincre.
It seems useless to me to try to convince you.

Il s'agit d'une histoire géniale.
It involves a fantastic story.

Il s'agit d'écrire une histoire en une semaine.
It has to do with writing a story in one week.

Other Impersonal Expressions

Other common impersonal expressions include **il vaut mieux** (*it's better, advisable*) and **il y a** (*there is, there are*). An impersonal expression can be followed by 1) **à** + infinitive (**il est difficile à** comprendre = *it's hard to understand*), 2) **de** + infinitive (**il est difficile de** comprendre les journaux = *it's hard to understand the newspapers*), 3) **que** + subject + indicative, 4) **que** + subject + subjunctive.

Typical uses of **être** + adjective:

il est dommage	*it's too bad*
il est bon	*it's good*
il est facile	*it's easy*
il est faux	*it's false*
il est honteux	*it's shameful*
il est injuste	*it's unfair*
il est peu probable	*it's not likely*
il est urgent	*it's urgent*
il est temps	*it's time*

Passive and Avoidance of the Passive

① La tour Eiffel **a** été construite par Gustave Eiffel.

② Ce plan de ville se lit facilement.

③ A Paris, on prend souvent le métro.

---

1. The Eiffel Tower was built by Gustave Eiffel. 2. This city map is easy to read.
3. In Paris, people often take the subway.

Only verbs with direct objects can form the passive voice. The passive is not very common in French; it is found primarily in literary French. Therefore, substitutes for the passive play an important role.

> Direct objects are sentence complements that receive the action of a transitive verb, with no intervening preposition.

Formation

These three sample sentences are typical active sentences with the following elements: subject (**Michel**), verb (**conduit**), and object (**une voiture**).

Subject	Verb	Object	
Michel	**conduit**	une voiture.	
Les allemands	**ont détruit**	la ville.	
L'employé	**fermera**	la porte	à 6 heures.

In French, the passive voice is always made up of some form of **être + past participle**. The participle agrees in gender and number with the noun it modifies. The agent (if one is mentioned) is introduced by **par**.

Subject	Verb		Agent
La voiture	**est conduite**		**par** Michel.
La ville	**a été détruite**		**par** les Allemands.
La porte	**sera fermée**	à 6 heures	(**par** l'employé).

141

Substitutes for the Passive

Use

Dans beaucoup de pays anglophones, **on roule** à gauche.
On a décidé d'augmenter la T.V.A.

Instead of using the passive, you can create active sentences with **on**. Such constructions are very popular in colloquial French.

Les cigarettes **se vendent** surtout dans les bureaux de tabac.
Le pastis **se boit** avec de l'eau et des glaçons.

Reflexive verbs are often used instead of the passive voice, especially when the agent is not mentioned and when a thing is involved.

Il **s'est fait voler** ses papiers.	*His papers were stolen.*
Elle **se fait offrir** un cadeau.	*She was offered a gift.*
Elle **s'est fait faire** une permanente.	*She got a permanent.*

A construction with **se faire** + infinitive can apply only to persons.

L'augmentation de la T.V.A. **sera l'objet d'**une violente discussion.

The construction **être l'objet de** is typical of journalese.

1. Rewrite the following sentences, using passive constructions. **

a) En Alsace, on parle aussi l'allemand.

  L'allemand est aussi parlé en Alsace   .

l'Alsace – *Alsace*

le siècle – *century*

b) Au 17ᵉ siècle, la France a occupé le pays.

                        .

c) Au 18ᵉ siècle, Vauban a construit des forteresses le long du Rhin.

                        .

une forteresse – *fortress*

d) En 1871, l'Empire d'Allemagne a annexé la province d'Alsace.

                        .

l'Empire d'Allemagne – *German Empire*
la province – *province*
un allié – *ally, one of the Allies*

e) En 1945, les alliés ont libéré l'Alsace des Allemands.

                        .

f) Et prochainement, la SNCF ouvrira une nouvelle ligne de TGV.

                        .

la SNCF – *French railroads*
le TGV – *high-speed train*

Negation

Tu as envie d'aller au cinéma ? – Oui.
①

Tu n'aimes pas aller au théâtre ? – Non.
②

Tu ne vas pas rentrer ce soir ? – Si.
③

---

1. Do you want to go to the movies? –Yes. 2. Don't you like to go to the theater? –No.
3. You're not going to go back home tonight, are you? –Yes.

oui, non, si

The answer to a question phrased in the negative is **non** if you agree with the questioner, and **si** if you are contradicting what he or she says.

> Tu as fait la vaisselle ? – **Oui.**
> Tu n'as pas fait un repas ? – **Non.**
> Tu n'as pas fait de courses ? – **Si.**

ne... pas, ne... plus, ne... jamais, ne... rien, ne... personne, ne... aucun

In French, negation is expressed with **ne** in combination with **pas**, **plus**, **jamais**, **rien**, **personne**, or **aucun**.

Je **ne** veux **pas** aller au cinéma.	*I don't want to go to the movies.*
Elle **ne** l'aime **plus**.	*She doesn't love him anymore.*
Ils **ne** sont **jamais** partis en vacances.	*They've never gone on vacation.*
On **n'**a **rien** mangé.	*We haven't eaten anything.*
Tu **n'**as vu **personne** ?	*Haven't you seen anybody?*
Jusqu'à présent, il **n'**a eu **aucun** accident.	*Until now he had never had an accident.*
Il **ne** connaît **aucune** fille.	*He doesn't know any girl at all.*

Placement of Negations

Il **ne** boit **pas**. Il **ne** buvait **pas**. Il **ne** boira **pas**. Il **n'**a pas **bu**. Il **ne** va **pas** boire. Il **ne** veut **pas** boire. **Ne** buvez **pas**.	**Ne... pas, ne... plus, ne... jamais**, and **ne... rien** enclose the conjugated verb (**boit, a, va, veut**, etc.) like a sandwich: **ne** precedes the verb and **pas / plus / jamais / rien** directly follow it.

Il **n'**en a **pas** bu.
Je **ne** lui ai **plus** parlé.
Elle **ne** m'a **jamais** pardonné.
Ils **ne** leur ont **rien** fait.

Pronouns are placed between **ne** and the conjugated verb.

▶ On pronouns, see the section beginning on p. 41

Je **ne** vois **personne**.
Nous **n'**avons vu **personne**.
Il **n'**a trouvé **aucun** logement.

With compound tenses, **personne** and **aucun** are placed after the past participle.

J'avais l'idée de **ne pas** venir.
Elle a l'intention de **ne plus** le voir.
Il espère **ne jamais** la revoir.

The negations directly precede a negated infinitive.

Je pense **ne** voir **personne**.
Il a peur de **ne** trouver **aucune** place.

With a negated infinitive, too, **personne** and **aucun** occupy a special position.

Il **ne** parle à **personne**.
Elle **ne** pense à **rien**.
Il **ne** parle à **aucune** fille.
Je **n'**ai besoin de **rien**.

Personne, **rien**, and **aucun** can also be indirect objects. In this case, they follow the preposition **à** or **de**.

Rien ne me manque.
Personne ne le sait.
Aucun ne lui téléphone.

Rien, **personne**, and **aucun** are the first element in the sentence if they are the subject of the sentence.

Negation of Nouns

Je n'aime pas les kiwis.

I don't like kiwis.

Pas behaves like an expression of quantity: It is not followed by the article, but only by **de**.

Il **ne** boit **pas** d'alcool.
Elle **n'**a **jamais** mangé de pommes.

With **être**, it is not the noun but the verb that is negated; therefore, the article is used here.

Ce **n'**est **pas** une orange, c'est une clémentine.
Ce **n'**est **pas** du jus, mais du vin.

After verbs that express emotion, such as **aimer**, **adorer**, **détester**, the article is used both in affirmative and in negative sentences.

Il **n'**aime **pas** la viande.
Je **ne** déteste **plus** les fruits.

Combined Negations

Negations such as "never again," "not yet," and "not always" are expressed as follows:

Elle **ne** parlera **plus jamais** à ses parents.
She will never speak to her parents again.

Il **n'**a **plus rien** dit.
He has said nothing more.

Elle **n'**a **plus vu** personne.
She has seen no one else.

Les professeurs **ne** sont **pas toujours** mauvais.
Teachers are not always bad.

Elle **n'**a **toujours pas** appris le français.
She still hasn't learned French.

Elle **n'**a **toujours rien** reçu.
She still has received nothing.

Je **n'**ai **toujours** reçu **aucune** nouvelle.
I still haven't received any news.

Je **ne** suis **pas encore** allée en France.
I still haven't gone to France.

In some contexts, **rien**, **personne**, and **aucune** are rendered as "anything," "anybody / anyone," and "ever."

Il n'a jamais **rien** dit de pareil.
He never said anything like that.

Je n'ai jamais fait du mal **à personne**.
I have never harmed anybody.

Personne ne saura **jamais** comment il est mort.
No one will ever know how he died.

Il est parti sans **rien** manger.
He left without eating anything.

Il s'est acheté une voiture sans demander **à personne**.
He bought himself a car without asking anyone.

du tout

Je n'ai pas du tout envie d'aller au cinéma.

I have no desire at all to go to the movies.

Ne... pas/**rien**/**plus** can be intensified by **du tout**. In this case, **du tout** follows the second part of the negation.

Il y a trois ans, il **n'a plus du tout** bu.
Three years ago he didn't drink at all anymore.

L'été dernier, il n'a fait **rien du tout**.
Last summer he didn't do anything at all.

non plus

The negation of **aussi** is **non plus**.

Moi, je **n'**irai **pas** à la fête. – Et moi, je **n'**irai **pas non plus**.
I'm not going to the party. – And I'm not going either.

Elle **n'**a **rien** remarqué. – **Lui non plus**, il **n'**a **rien** remarqué.
She didn't notice anything. – Nor did he, he didn't notice anything either.

ne... que and *seulement*

In most cases, **ne... que** and **seulement** are interchangeable. They can be rendered in English as "only," "solely," or "(nothing) but."

Je **ne** bois **que** de l'eau.   Je bois **seulement** de l'eau.
Elle **n'**a **que** quinze ans.   Elle a **seulement** quinze ans.

If **seulement + verb** is followed by a subordinate clause introduced by **que**, then **seulement** cannot be replaced by **ne... que**.

Il a **seulement** dit qu'elle était partie.

ne... ni... ni

Ni... ni is the equivalent of English "neither ... nor."
Ni... ni can be used before adjectives, nouns, or infinitives.

Il **n'**est **ni** beau **ni** intelligent.
Il **ne** sait **ni** lire **ni** écrire.
Ni le cinéma **ni** le théâtre **ne** l'intéressent.

> Although the verb is not negated in English "neither ... nor" constructions, in French it must be preceded by **ne** or **n'**.

Negation

1. Michel is stubborn. Negate the following, using **ne... pas de**. *

a) Tu veux une orange?

Non, _je ne veux pas d'orange._

b) Tu veux peut-être une pomme ?

Non, _____

c) Tu aimerais une glace ?

Non, _____

d) Tu veux peut-être un nouveau T-shirt ?

Non, _____

e) Alors, on fait un voyage en Espagne ?

_____

f) Eh bien, il te faut une nouvelle amie ?

_____

2. Answer the sentences in the negative. **

a) Voulez-vous prendre un café ?

Non, _je ne veux pas prendre de café_ .

b) Tu as mangé un sandwich ?

Non, _____ .

c) Tu veux boire quelque chose ?

Non, _____ .

d) Tu as déjà parlé à ton professeur ?

Non, _____ .

e) Tu vas inviter quelqu'un pour ce soir ?

Non, _____ .

f) Tu as vu quelque chose ?

Non, _____ .

g) Tu manges de la viande ?

Non, _____ .

h) C'est ton ami ?

   Non, _____ .

i) Vous adorez la musique ?

   Non, _____ .

j) Il te manque quelque chose ?

   Non, _____ .

k) Tu feras encore un voyage ?

   Non, _____ .

l) Vous avez vu Barbara ou Michel ?

   Non, _____ .

m) C'est du fromage ?

   Non, _____ .

n) Il a dit encore quelque chose ?

   Non, _____ .

o) Est-ce qu'il a enfin trouvé une femme ?

   Non, _____ .

p) Est-ce qu'elle n'a pas encore parlé à ses parents ?

   Non, _____ .

q) Est-ce qu'elle a parlé encore à quelqu'un ?

   Non, _____ .

r) Est-ce que vous avez regardez toujours la télé ?

   Non, _____ .

s) Tu as déjà passé ton permis de conduire ?

   Non, _____ .

t) Christine ne viendra pas. Et toi, tu viendras ?

   Non, _____ .

Negation

3. Match the questions with the correct answers. *

a) Tu as déjà écrit à ton amie ?   Non, je n'ai rien acheté.

b) Est-ce que tu vas à Paris ?   Non, elle n'a plus rien dit.

c) Tu as acheté quelque chose   Non, je ne lui ai pas encore
   pour ce soir ?   écrit.

d) Tu as écrit ce poème ?   Non, je n'ai vu personne.

e) Tu as vu quelqu'un dans la rue ?   Non, elle n'a pas du tout changé.

f) Est-ce qu'elle a dit encore   Non, je n'en mange plus.
   quelque chose ?

g) Tu manges de la viande ?   Non, je n'y vais pas.

h) Est-ce qu'elle a changé ?   Non, pas celui-ci.

Indirect Discourse

1. Mon mari m'a demandé si j'avais vu la belle lune.

2. Et il m'a dit qu'il m'aimait.

---

1. *My husband asked me whether I had seen the beautiful moon.*
2. *And he told me that he loved me.*

Formation of Indirect Discourse

As in English, the pronouns and determiners must be changed in indirect discourse. Naturally, the endings of the verbs must change here as well. The adjustments are always made from the perspective of the speaker.

> **direct discourse**
>
> Ma mère demande : « **Tu as** déjà fait **tes** devoirs ? »
> Je réponds : « J'aimerais que **tu m'aides** un peu. »
>
> **indirect discourse**
>
> Ma mère demande si **j'ai** déjà fait **mes** devoirs.
> Je réponds que j'aimerais qu'**elle m'aide** un peu.

1. Introduction of Subordinate Clauses

After **dire**, **répondre**, **ajouter**, etc., the subordinate clause is introduced by **que**.

Je dis: « Je m'ennuie. »
Je dis **que** je m'ennuie.

> **!** This is a basic rule: There is no **est-ce que** in indirect discourse.

Formation of Indirect Discourse

A decision question (yes-or-no question) after **demander** is introduced by **si**.

> Mon frère demande: « Tu resteras à la maison ? »
> Mon frère demande **si** je resterai à la maison.

The question word **que** used in direct discourse becomes **ce que** in indirect discourse.

> Moi, je veux savoir : « **Qu'**est-ce qu'on fera le week-end ? »
> Moi, je veux savoir **ce qu'**on fera le week-end.

> Question words used in probe questions: quand, où, qui, quel, quoi.

The question words in a probe question (information-seeking question) are retained in indirect discourse.

> Mon père demande : « **Quand** est-ce que tu rentreras ? »
> Mon père demande **quand** je rentrerai.

> Ma mère veut savoir : « **Avec qui** est-ce que tu passeras la soirée ? »
> Ma mère veut savoir **avec qui** je passerai la soirée.

> Mon père demande : « **Où** est-ce que vous irez ? »
> Mon père demande **où** nous irons.

2. Change of Tense

If the verb that introduces the indirect discourse is in one of the past tenses (for example, "Il a dit que ... "), then the tense in the subordinate clause must be changed. Then all verb forms have only the following endings:

-ais	**-ions**
-ais	**-iez**
-ait	**-aient**

The following rules for recasting apply:

direct discourse	indirect discourse	
present	imperfect	fais**ait**
compound past	pluperfect	av**ait** fait
simple future	present conditional	fer**ait**
future perfect	past conditional	aur**ait** fait

The other tenses are retained:

direct discourse	indirect discourse	
imperfect	imperfect	fais**ait**
pluperfect	pluperfect	av**ait** fait
present conditional	present conditional	fer**ait**
past conditional	past conditional	aur**ait** fait

With a past tense verb that triggers indirect discourse, **demain** is replaced with **le lendemain**, **hier** with **la veille**, **aujourd'hui** with **ce jour-là**, and **ce soir** with **ce soir-là**.

> Il m'a demandé : « Qu'est-ce que tu as fait **hier** ? »
> Il m'a demandé ce que j'avais fait **la veille**.

> Et il voulait savoir : « Qu'est-ce que tu vas faire **demain** ? »
> Et il voulait savoir ce que j'allais faire **le lendemain**.

> Et ma mère a demandé : « Tu as déjà fait tes devoirs **aujourd'hui** ? »
> Et ma mère a demandé si j'avais déjà fait mes devoirs **ce jour-là**.

This is true only if the verb triggering indirect discourse is in a past tense. With other tenses, the expressions of time remain unchanged.

Practice and Application

Indirect Discourse

1. In the following examples of indirect discourse, the conjunctions **si** and **que** are missing. The verb forms are missing as well. Fill in the blanks with the words required. *

a) Mon ami dit _qu'_ il m' ___aime___ . (aimer)

b) Et il ajoute _____ il m' _____ (aimer) encore dans 20 ans.

c) Il me demande tous les jours _____ je _____ (ne pas en avoir) un autre.

d) Moi, je précise _____ je _____ (ne pas en voir) d'autres depuis que je le connais.

e) Et je lui demande _____ il _____ (faire) la connaissance d'une autre fille.

f) Lui, il répond _____ il _____ (ne jamais me quitter).

2. Change the following sentences to indirect discourse. In a statement, use the verb **dire** to introduce the indirect discourse, and in a question, use the verb **demander**. **

Ma mère dit que … / Ma mère demande si …

a) « Est-ce que tu as déjà un petit ami ? »

   Elle demande si j'ai déjà un petit ami.

b) « Je veux que tu fasses tes devoirs. »

   _____

c) « Tu ne sortiras pas demain. »

   _____

d) « Je me sens mieux si tu restes à la maison. »

   _____

e) « Est-ce que tu as déjà rendu visite à tes grands-parents ? »

   _____

f) « Qu'est-ce que tu vas offrir à ton père pour son anniversaire ? »

   _____

g) « Pourrais-tu m'aider à faire la vaisselle ? »

   _____

3. Complete the following indirect discourse by adding the appropriate verb forms. The verbs that introduce the indirect discourse are in the past! *

a) Ma grand-mère voulait savoir si __j'avais déjà fait__ mes devoirs.
(faire)

b) Elle m'a demandé si j' _____ (avoir) une petite amie.

c) Elle a dit qu'elle _____ (être mariée) depuis 40 ans.

d) Elle a ajouté qu'elle _____ (faire) la connaissance de mon grand-père pendant son voyage en Espagne.

e) Et elle a dit qu'elle ne le _____ (quitter) jamais.

f) Et elle a précisé qu'elle l'_____ (aimer) toujours.

g) Elle m'a demandé si je _____ (penser) comme elle.

4. Madame Dutour is going on a trip soon. Her husband is asking her a few questions. Put the following sentences in indirect discourse. The verbs that introduce the indirect discourse are in the present tense. **

Monsieur Dutour veut savoir de sa femme …

a) « Est-ce que tu vas m'envoyer une carte postale ? »

   __Il veut savoir si elle va lui envoyer une carte postale.__

b) « Tu m'appelleras de Paris ? »

   _____

c) « Je peux te téléphoner de temps en temps ? »

   _____

d) « Tu m'apporteras un petit cadeau ? »

   _____

e) « Est-ce que ta sœur va t'accompagner ? »

   _____

f) « Tu ne vas pas t'ennuyer sans moi ? »

   _____

g) « Qu'est-ce que je vais faire sans toi ? »

   _____

Indirect Discourse

5. Change the following direct discourse to the past. Use the appropriate verbs to introduce indirect discourse.

Mon professeur m'a demandé / voulait savoir / a dit / a ajouté...

a) « Est-ce que tu as fait tes devoirs ? »

   Mon professeur m'a demandé si j'avais fait mes devoirs.

b) « Quand est-ce que tu les as faits ? »

c) « Est-ce que quelqu'un t'a aidé à les faire ? »

d) « Pourrais-tu me répondre correctement ? »

e) « Je ne crois pas que tu puisses me donner une traduction correcte. »

f) « Pour cette traduction tu vas avoir une mauvaise note. »

g) « J'appellerai tes parents aujourd'hui même. »

h) « Demain tu me rendras cette lettre. »

i) « La prochaine fois, tu vas voir le directeur. »

j) « Qu'est-ce que tu fais pendant tout l'après-midi ? »

k) « Tu as déjà pensé à ton avenir ? »

l) « Il y a trente ans, un élève comme toi n'aurait pas travaillé comme ça. »

Adjectives

C'est un bel hôtel avec une atmosphère agréable. ①

Oui, Madame Le Grand a vraiment de beaux hôtels. ②

1. *It's a pretty hotel with a pleasant atmosphere.*
2. *Yes, Madame Le Grand has really nice hotels.*

Masculine and Feminine Adjectives

The adjective agrees in number and gender with the noun it modifies. In some cases, the masculine and feminine adjectives are identical in form. Usually, however, they are different.

Basic Rules for Formation of the Feminine Form

1. Basic Rule

The feminine form is formed by adding an **-e** to the masculine form. This is the first basic rule for formation of the feminine form of the adjective.

Il est **petit**.	un rôle **important**
Elle est **petite**.	une question **importante**
un **mauvais** acteur	un fromage **français**
la **mauvaise** route	la langue **française**
un auteur **américain**	
une actrice **américaine**	

> Other examples: joli, nu, vrai, spécial, clair, extérieur, direct, suspect, droit, étonnant, intelligent, froid, chaud, laid, profond, grand, allemand, espagnol, anglais, chinois, gris

2. Basic Rule

If the masculine form already ends in **-e**, then no further change is made in the feminine form.

un travail **difficile**	du vin **ordinaire**
une opération **difficile**	une personne **ordinaire**

un fromage **suisse**
la Confédération **suisse**

Other examples: facile, rare, sévère, pauvre, réalisable, rougeâtre, pittoresque, lisible, géométrique, égoïste, belge, russe, utile

Special Rules

-c	▶ -que:	un jardin **public**
		l'opinion **publique**
		turc – turque
		grec – grecque
-eur	▶ -eure:	un escalier **extérieur**
		une serrure **extérieure**
		meilleur – meilleure
		antérieur – antérieure
		intérieur - intérieure
-eur	▶ -euse:	un aspect **trompeur**
		une apparence **trompeuse**
		menteur – menteuse
		rêveur – rêveuse
		prometteur – prometteuse
-teur	▶ -trice:	un député **conservateur**
		une politique **conservatrice**
		créateur – créatrice
		destructeur – destructrice
		moteur – motrice

-f	▶ -ve:	un pont **neuf** une idée **neuve**
		actif – active, vif – vive juif – juive, naïf – naïve
-el	▶ -elle:	un teint **naturel** de l'eau minérale **naturelle**
		tel – telle, réel – réelle individuel – individuelle
-eil	▶ -eille:	en **pareil** cas à **pareille** heure
-en -on	▶ -enne: ▶ -onne:	un meuble **ancien** une amitié **ancienne**
		un **bon** résultat une **bonne** excuse
		moyen – moyenne breton – bretonne européen – européenne
-er	▶ -ère:	un vin **léger** une matière **légère**
		premier – première cher – chère fier – fière
-et	▶ -ette:	un film **muet** une femme **muette**
		coquet – coquette net – nette
-et	▶ -ète:	un train **complet** une œuvre **complète**
		discret – discrète inquiet – inquiète

! The feminine form of bref is br**è**ve.

! Note: Adjectives ending in **-al** and **-il** are derived in accordance with Basic Rule 1: amical – amicale, civil – civile

Masculine and Feminine Adjectives

-s	▸ -sse:	le foie **gras** la matière **grasse** bas – basse, gros – grosse épais – épaisse
-x	▸ -se:	un chemin **dangereux** une zone **dangereuse** jaloux – jalouse curieux – curieuse

Exceptions:
doux – douce
faux – fausse
roux – rousse

Exceptions

aigu – *acute, sharp*

masculine	feminine	masculine	feminine
aigu	aiguë	hébreu	hébraïque
blanc	blanche	long	longue
favori	favorite	paysan	paysanne
frais	fraîche	sec	sèche
gentil	gentille		

Adjectives with Two Masculine Forms

The second singular form exists only for the adjectives **beau**, **vieux**, and **nouveau**.

Three masculine adjectives have a second form <u>in the singular</u>. It <u>precedes</u> nouns that begin with a vowel or with h. If the adjective follows the noun, the normal masculine form is used.

masculine	feminine
un **beau** studio un **bel** appartement un appartement **beau** et pas cher	une **belle** maison
un **vieux** monsieur un **vieil** homme un homme **vieux** et malade	une **vieille** femme
un **nouveau** pantalon un **nouvel** anorak un anorak **nouveau** et chic	une **nouvelle** jupe

Formation of the Plural

Hier, j'ai rencontré des gens aimables.

Yesterday I met some nice people.

Basic Rule

The plural of adjectives normally ends in **-s** (basic rule). The same rules apply as for the formation of noun plurals.

▶ On forming noun plurals, see p. 17

masculine	feminine
un grand appartement	une grande maison
de grands appartements	de grandes maisons
petit – petits	petite – petites
difficile – difficiles	difficile – difficiles
blanc – blancs	blanche – blanches

1. Special Rule

Masculine adjectives ending in **-al** or **-eau** add **-aux** or **-eaux** to form the plural.

masculine	feminine
un signe amical	une voix amicale
des signes amicaux	des voix amicales
un beau studio	une belle maison
de beaux studios	de belles maisons
un bel appartement	
de beaux appartements	

Exception:
The masculine forms **banal**, **fatal**, **final**, and **naval** have regular plurals ending in **-als**.

2. Special Rule

Masculine singular forms ending in **-s** and **-x** do not change in the plural.

masculine	feminine
un gros chien	une grosse valise
de gros chiens	de grosses valises

un chemin dangereu**x**	une zone dangereuse
des chemins dangereu**x**	des zones dangereuses
gris – gris	grise – grises
doux – doux	douce – douces

> In colloquial French, however, **des** is quite often used.

If the adjective precedes the noun, then the plural of the indefinite article is **de**.

un gros chien   but: un chien dangereux
de gros chiens   **des** chiens dangereux

Special Features of the Agreement of Adjectives

> C'est une jupe chic !

That's a cute skirt!

Invariable Adjectives

Nouns that are used as adjectives are invariable.

un pantalon azur   une robe azur
des pantalons azur   des robes azur

> ▸ abricot, aubergine, azur, cerise, citron, kaki, marron, olive, orange, paille, chic, snob, bon marché

Compound Adjectives

Basic Rule

If two adjectives are joined by a hyphen to create a compound (adjective + adjective), both are changed.

> sourd-muet – *deaf-mute, deaf and dumb*

un enfant **sourd-muet**   une fille **sourde-muette**
des enfants **sourds-muets**   des femmes **sourdes-muettes**

> ▸ social-démocrate, chrétien-démocrate, libéral-démocrate

Special Rules

If the first of the two compound adjectives ends in **-o** or designates a point of the compass, it is not changed.

    un film **franco-allemand**   l'amitié **franco-allemande**
    des films **franco-allemands**   les relations **franco-allemandes**

The same rule governs compounds of which the first part is a preposition.

    un pays **sous-développé**   une région **sous-développée**
    des pays **sous-développés**   des régions **sous-développées**

sous-développé –
underdeveloped

> ▸ germano-français, nord-américain, sud-africain, avant-dernier

Color adjectives are invariable if they consist of more than one word.

    un pantalon **bleu ciel**   une chemise **bleu ciel**
    des pantalons **bleu ciel**   des chemises **bleu ciel**

> ▸ bleu marine, bleu vert, bleu clair, bleu foncé

Demi, **nu**, and **nouveau** remain unchanged if they precede the noun and are linked to it with a hyphen.

    le **demi**-monde   une **demi**-heure

    un **nouveau**-né
    des **nouveau**-nés

Grand has no feminine form if it precedes the noun and is linked to it by a hyphen.

    le **grand**-père   la **grand**-mère
    les **grands**-pères   les **grands**-mères

    la **grand**-tante   ne... pas **grand**-chose
    les **grands**-tantes

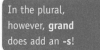

In the plural, however, **grand** does add an **-s**!

Special Features of the Agreement of Adjectives

Use

Il est **vieux**.	**Elle** est **vieille**.
Ils sont **vieux**.	**Elles** sont **vieilles**.

The adjective can be linked with **être**. Then it modifies the subject and agrees with it in number and gender.

Il est devenu **vieux**.	
Elle est devenue **vieille**.	devenir, paraître, sembler,
Les jours me semblent **courts**.	demeurer, rester, faire
Les hommes demeurent **libres**.	(meaning "to act")
Ils sont restés **seuls**.	
Elle fait **vieille**.	

A few other verbs perform the same function as **être**: The adjective modifies the subject.

Je **le** trouve **beau**.	
Il **la** trouve **belle**.	
Je **les** crois **partis**.	trouver, croire, estimer, juger,
Vous pouvez **vous** estimer	déclarer, se dire, se prétendre,
heureux.	se sentir, se montrer, s'avérer,
Elle **se** dit **intelligente**.	rendre, avoir l'air
Elle **se** prétend **jeune**.	
Ils **se** sentent **seuls**.	

If an adjective modifies a <u>direct object</u>, it agrees with it in number and gender.

Il a acheté un **grand appartement**.	Il a acheté une **grande maison**.
Il a acheté un **costume gris**.	Il a acheté une **cravate noire**.

The adjective can also refer directly to a noun, independently of a verb. Then it agrees with that noun in number and gender.

Placement Before or After the Noun

C'était un film intéressant.

It was an interesting film.

Placement After the Noun

Most adjectives are positioned after the noun. This includes adjectives that denote the following properties:

colors, shapes, appearance:	une voiture **rouge** des cheveux **blonds** une table **ronde** une maison **neuve**
physical, bodily, or intellectual qualities:	un climat **sec** une valise **lourde** une femme **mince** un homme **sage**
nationality, religion, economics, societal matters, politics, culture:	l'économie **française** la situation **actuelle**
geography, time:	les pays **nordiques** un rapport **annuel**
participles used adjectivally:	un chemin **barré** un travail **fatigant**

Multisyllabic adjectives are always placed after the word modified:

un but **irréalisable**	une lettre **illisible**

Placement Before the Noun

Only a few <u>short</u> adjectives usually are placed before the noun.

un **petit** jardin **bonne** nouvelle	une **meilleure** idée une **jolie** fille	une **mauvaise** surprise

petit, bon, mauvais, beau, joli, vieux, gros, bref, haut, bas, meilleur, moindre

Placement After the Noun

("B" stands for "meaning of adjective placed before the noun"; "A" stands for "meaning of adjective placed after the noun.")

In dictionaries, look for an indication of a change in meaning related to placement.

Some commonly used adjectives have different meanings depending on where they are placed. The most important adjectives in this group are:

une **ancienne** amie	B: *former*
une ville **ancienne**	A: *old*
une **brave** femme	B: *honest, good*
une femme **brave**	A: *brave, courageous*
un **certain** Michel	B: *certain, particular*
une date **certaine**	A: *definite, certain, sure*
cher ami	B: *dear*
des chaussures **chères**	A: *expensive*
un **court** séjour	B: *short* (time)
une jupe **courte**	A: *short* (space)
le **dernier** visiteur	B: *last*
la semaine **dernière**	A: *previous*
un **grand** homme	B: *important, great*
un homme **grand**	A: *big*
un **jeune** homme	B: *young*
un homme **jeune**	A: *youthful*
une **longue** maladie	B: *long* (time)
une robe **longue**	A: *long* (space)
une **nouvelle** voiture	B: *new, different*
une voiture **nouvelle**	A: *new* (brand new)
une **pauvre** fille	B: *poor, pitiful*
une fille **pauvre**	A: *poor, impoverished*
mes **propres** paroles	B: *own*
une assiette **propre**	A: *clean*
un **rare** esprit	B: *unusual, extraordinary*
une plante **rare**	A: *rare*
un **sacré** menteur	B: *goddamn*
les livres **sacrés**	A: *holy, sacred*
Saint-Michel	B: Saint + first name
l'Histoire **sainte**	A: *holy, blessed*
un **sale** travail	B: *lousy, mean*
des mains **sales**	A: *dirty*

le **seul** ami	B: *only, sole*
un homme **seul**	A: *lonely, single*
vêtu d'un **simple** pull	B: *mere*
un homme **simple**	A: *simple, naïve*
un **triste** état	B: *dreary*
une histoire **triste**	A: *sad*
du **vrai** bois	B: *real, genuine*
une histoire **vraie**	A: *true*

> **vrai**
> Before the noun:
> *authentic, genuine*
> After the noun: *true,*
> in the sense of *not*
> *made up / false*

The Placement of Two Adjectives

Both adjectives can retain the position they occupy when appearing singly. But if two adjectives occur before or after the noun, they are linked with **et**.

> un **mauvais** auteur **américain**
> une **grande et belle** femme
> un hôtel **tranquille et confortable**

Both adjectives can also be positioned after the noun, even if they would be before it if used singly. In this case, too, they must be linked with **et**.

> une femme **grande et belle**
> une maison **grande et vieille**
> des vacances **longues et belles**

Comparison of Adjectives

1. La chemise rose est **aussi chère que** la chemise grise.

2. Le jean rouge est **plus cher que** le jean jaune.

3. Le tee-shirt noir est **moins cher que** le tee-shirt blanc.

---

1. The pink shirt is just as expensive as the gray shirt. 2. The red jeans are more expensive than the black jeans. 3. The black T-shirt is cheaper than the white T-shirt.

Formation of the Comparative

Comparatives are constructed according to the following pattern: "Equality" is expressed by **aussi** + adjective + **que**.

> Michel est **aussi grand que** Paul.
> Emma est **aussi sportive qu'**Anne.

"Superiority" is expressed by **plus** + adjective + **que**.

> Eric est **plus grand que** Pierre.
> Annick est **plus sportive qu'**Alain.

"Inferiority" is expressed by **moins** + adjective + **que.**

> Pierre est **moins grand qu'**Eric.
> Alain est **moins sportif qu'**Annick.

Formation of the Superlative

The superlative is expressed by using **le / la / les plus** + adjective,

> Quelle est la fille **la plus sportive** ?
> Annick est la fille **la plus sportive**.

or by using **le / la / les moins** + adjective.

> Quel est le garçon **le moins grand** ?
> Pierre est **le moins grand**.

Irregular Comparative Forms

The adjectives **bon**, **mauvais**, and **petit** have irregular forms of comparison.

> **Plus mauvais** and **plus petit** also exist.

!

bon(s)	meilleur(s)	le / les meilleur(s)
bonne(s)	meilleure(s)	la / les meilleure(s)
mauvais	pire(s)	le / les pire(s)
mauvaise(s)	pire(s)	la / les pire(s)
petit(s)	moindre(s)	le / les moindre(s)
petite(s)	moindre(s)	la / les moindre(s)

> Ce vin est **bon**.
> Celui-ci est **meilleur** (que l'autre).
> Et celui-là est **le meilleur** de tous.
> Mes **meilleurs** vœux !

> Cet homme est **mauvais**.
> Les hommes sont **pires que** les femmes.
> Le travail est **la pire des choses**.

> Voilà ses **petits** problèmes.
> Aujourd'hui, ses problèmes sont **moindres** qu'ils ne l'étaient hier.
> Et demain, il va nous expliquer **les moindres détails** de ses problèmes.

Practice and Application

1. Fill in the missing masculine or feminine forms of the adjectives. *

aigu – *acute, sharp*
public – *public*
vive – *live, lively*
amer – *bitter*
net – *neat, tidy*
jalouse – *jealous*
bon marché – *inexpensive, cheap*
gras - *fatty, greasy*

a) froid _____froide_____   b) _____ rare

c) _____ secrète   d) européen _____

e) faux _____   f) aigu _____

g) public _____   h) _____ facile

i) _____ réelle   j) _____ fraîche

k) turc _____   l) grec _____

m) _____ vive   n) amer _____

o) net _____   p) gros _____

q) blanc _____   r) _____ jalouse

s) suisse _____   t) _____ russe

u) bon marché _____   v) citron _____

w) complet _____   x) gras _____

2. Fill in the missing singular or plural forms of the adjectives. *

fatal – *fateful, fatal*
gris – *gray*
amical – *friendly*

	masculine singular	masculine plural	feminine singular	feminine plural
a)	_mauvais_	mauvais	_____	_____
b)	fatal	_____	_____	_____
c)	_____	gris	_____	_____
d)	long	_____	_____	_____
e)	amical	_____	_____	_____
f)	_____	beaux	_____	_____
g)	_____	vieux	_____	_____
h)	dur	_____	_____	_____
i)	gentil	_____	_____	_____
j)	_____	_____	_____	fraîches
k)	européen	_____	_____	_____
l)	sec	_____	_____	_____

3. Decide whether the adjectives in the following sentences should
be placed before or after the noun. Make sure they agree with the
word modified! **

a) L'année dernière, nous avons acheté une ___nouvelle___

maison _____.

b) Elle a une _____ salle de séjour _____, une

_____ salle de bains _____ et quatre

_____ chambres _____.

c) C'était un _____ travail _____ pour nettoyer

cette _____ maison _____ .

d) Ma _____ mère _____ !

e) Elle a fait ce _____ travail _____ jusqu'au

_____ moment _____ avant de déménager.

f) Mais enfin, après de _____ travaux _____ ,

on avait une _____ maison _____ .

g) Le _____ défaut _____ de cette maison, c'est

sa _____ isolation _____ .

a) ~~nouveau~~

b) grand, minuscule,
petit

c) fatigant, vieux

d) pauvre

e) sale, dernier

e) long, propre

f) seul, mauvais

4. Put the words provided together to form sentences. Pay attention to
the adjective endings and to the placement of the adjectives. ***

a) je – acheter – ancien – une voiture

  J'achète une voiture ancienne.

b) il – avoir – brun – des cheveux

_____

c) elle – faire – léger – une sauce

_____

d) ils – faire partie de – catholique – l'église

_____

e) tu – écrire avec – gauche – la main

_____

f) je – lire – gros – un livre

_____

Adjectives

g) vous – raconter – bref – une histoire

_____

h) elle – arriver avec – cassé – jambe

_____

i) ils – préférer – turc – la nourriture

_____

j) je – voir – franco-allemand – une pièce

_____

k) elle – contacter – certain – Yves

_____

l) elles – porter – long – des robes

_____

m) il – s'acheter – nouveau *(fabrikneu)* – une voiture

_____

n) elle – mener – simple – une vie

_____

o) ils – avoir passé l'examen – dernier – la semaine

_____

p) il - mon – être – ami – seul *(einziger)*

_____

q) mes parents – appartement – avoir – grand

_____

5. Rewrite the sentences below, using the comparative form of each adjective provided. **

a) Le château de Chenonceaux date du 16ᵉ siècle. Celui de Versailles date du 17ᵉ siècle. (vieux)

   Le château de Chenonceaux est plus vieux que celui de Versailles.

b) Monique mesure 1 m 80. Florence mesure 1 m 70. (grand)

_____

c) M. Dutour a acheté sa voiture en 1997. M. Floret a acheté la sienne en 1996. (neuf)

_____

_____

d) Une chambre à l'Hôtel de Provence coûte 150 euros, à l'Hôtel de Normandie seulement 120 euros. (cher)

_____

_____

e) Voilà les résultats de l'examen : Olivier a 85 points, Marc a 78 points. (bon)

_____

f) Barbara crie de temps en temps. Michel crie tous les jours. (mauvais)

_____

Adverbs

1. Normalement, Anne travaille sérieusement.

2. Mais aujourd'hui, elle ne travaille pas bien parce qu'elle est fatiguée.

---

1. Normally, Anne works conscientiously.
2. But today she's not doing good work because she is tired.

! French adjectives and adverbs almost always differ in form.

In French, you have to distinguish between adjectives and adverbs because they have different forms.
French adverbs either end in **-ment** or have a special form that differs from the corresponding adjective.

Use

▶ See p. 164

Elle est courageuse.
Ils sont rapides.
Elle est devenue vieille.

▌ With **être** and a small number of other verbs (see p. 164), the adjective is used because in sentences with **être**, people or things are being described by adjectives (What is someone or something like?).

Elle travaille **courageusement**.
Ils sont partis **rapidement**.
Elle mange **bien**.

▌ In the examples above, verbs are being modified (How is an action occurring?). Therefore **adverbs** are required, and they differ in form from adjectives.

C'est **extrêmement** simple.
Elle est **sérieusement** blessée.
Elle est **très** contente.

■ Adverbs also can modify, or qualify the meaning of, adjectives
(How pretty / good / bad ... is something or someone?).

Elle mange **très** lentement.
J'y suis allé **assez** régulièrement.
Ils boivent **beaucoup** trop.

■ Adverbs also can modify other adjectives
(**lentement**, **régulièrement**, **trop**).

Formation of Adverbs Ending in *-ment*

Notre hôtel est entièrement climatisé.

Our hotel is completely air-conditioned.

Basic Rules

The ending **-ment** is added to the feminine form of the adjective.

heureux, -euse	▶ **heureusement**
rare	▶ **rarement**
complet, -ète	▶ **complètement**

Some adjectives that end in **-e** have an adverb ending in **-ément**.

profond, e	▶ **profondément**
énorme	▶ **énormément**
précis, e	▶ **précisément**
conforme	▶ **conformément**
commun	▶ **communément**

With some adjectives whose masculine form ends in a vowel, the **-e** is
omitted in the adverb.

vrai, e	▶ **vraiment**
absolu, e	▶ **absolument**
poli, e	▶ **poliment**

Exception:
gai – gaiement or
gaiment

Placement of Adverbs Ending in -ment

Exceptions:
lent – lentement,
présent –
présentement,
véhément –
véhémentement

Adjectives ending in **-ant** or **-ent** usually form the adverb by adding **-amment** or **-emment**.

constant, e	▶ **constamment**
suffisant, e	▶ **suffisamment**
prudent, e	▶ **prudemment**

Special Forms

Some adjectives form unusual adverbs that cannot be derived:

bon, bonne	▶ **bien**
meilleur, e	▶ **mieux**
mauvais, e	▶ **mal**
bref, brève	▶ **brièvement**
gentil, gentille	▶ **gentiment**
journalier, -ière	▶ **journellement**
rapide	▶ **rapidement / vite**

Placement of Adverbs Ending in *-ment* That Are Not Derivatives

Use

An adverb ending in **-ment** is placed as follows:

Elle travaille **sérieusement**.   Elle travaillera **sérieusement**.

- with simple tenses, after the conjugated form of the verb.

Elle ne travaille pas **sérieusement**.

- with a negated verb, after the second element of negation (**pas, plus**).

Elle a travaillé **sérieusement**.   Elle va travailler **sérieusement**.

- with compound tenses, usually after the past participle or after the infinitive.

Heureusement, dans trois semaines je serai en vacances.
Malheureusement, j'ai encore beaucoup de travail à faire.

- at the beginning of the sentence, when it refers to the entire sentence.

Comparatives of Adverbs

> Ma fille travaille plus sérieusement que mon fils.

My daughter works more conscientiously than my son.

Basic Rule

"Equality" is expressed with **aussi** + adverb + **que**.

Il travaille **aussi** sérieusement **qu'**elle.
(… just as conscientiously as …)

"Superiority" is expressed with **plus** + adverb + **que**.

Elle travaille **plus** sérieusement **que** son frère.
(… more conscientiously than …)

"Inferiority" is expressed with **moins** + adverb + **que**.

Il parle **moins** bien **qu'**elle.
(… less well than …)

The **superlative** degree of the adverb is formed with **le plus…** or **le moins…**

Il parle **le plus** vite.   Il raisonne **le moins** logiquement.

> With "le plus" or "le moins," no distinction is made between genders!

Special Forms

Special forms of **bien**

aussi bien (que)	Elle parle **aussi bien que** lui.
mieux (que)	Elle parle **mieux que** lui.
moins bien (que)	Elle parle **moins bien que** lui.
le mieux	Elle parle **le mieux**.

Special forms of **peu**

aussi peu (que)	Je le vois **aussi peu qu'**elle.
moins (que)	Je le vois **moins qu'**elle.
plus (que)	Je le vois **plus qu'**elle.
le moins	Je le vois **le moins**.

moins (que) –
less often (than)
plus (que) –
more often (than)
le plus – *most often*

autant (que) – *just as much (as)*
plus (que) – *more (than)*
moins (que) – *less (than)*
le plus – *most*

Special forms of **beaucoup**

autant (que)	Il parle **autant qu'**elle.
plus (que)	Il parle **plus qu'**elle.
moins (que)	Il parle **moins qu'**elle.
le plus	Il parle **le plus**.

Note: If **plus** or **moins** is used to introduce an expression of quantity, **que** is replaced with **de**.

Elle gagne **plus de** 2000 euros par mois.

Adjectives Used as Adverbs

Some adjectives are used as adverbs and thus are invariable. The most important phrases are:

Achetez français.	*Buy French (products).*
Parlez plus fort.	*Speak louder.*
Parlez bas.	*Speak softer.*
Votez socialiste.	*Vote (for the) Socialist (Party).*
Il faut **marcher droit.**	*You must walk straight.*
Ils **gagnent gros.**	*They earn a lot.*
Vous **allez tout droit.**	*Go straight ahead.*
Elle **travaille dur.**	*She works hard.*
Elle **chante faux / juste.**	*She sings off-key / on-key.*
Ça **sonne faux / juste.**	*That sounds wrong / right.*
Ça **coûte cher.**	*That's expensive.*
Ça **sent bon / mauvais.**	*That smells good / bad.*

Adverbs Used as Adjectives

The adverbs **bien, mal,** and **mieux** can also be used as adjectives.

Ce restaurant est **bien.**	*This restaurant is good.*
Ce restaurant est **mieux.**	*This restaurant is better.*
Ce restaurant n'est **pas mal.**	*This restaurant is not bad.*
Je connais beaucoup de **gens bien.**	*I know many good people.*
Je voudrais manger **quelque chose de bien.**	*I would like to eat something good.*
Elle n'a **rien fait de mal.**	*She has done nothing bad.*
Il n'a pas fait **grand-chose de bien.**	*He has not done much good.*

très, *beaucoup*, *bien*, and *tout*

Dès maintenant, je vais travailler très sérieusement.

From now on, I'm going to work very conscientiously.

Très is used:

– before adjectives:

Cet appartement est **très grand**.   English meaning: *very*

– before adverbs:

Il se vend **très facilement**.   English meaning: *very*

- in phrases with **avoir** in which there is a noun without an article.

J'ai **très faim** et **très soif**.   English meaning: *very*

Beaucoup is used:

– with verbs:

Cet auteur me **plaît beaucoup**.   English meaning: *very much*

– before comparatives:

Il est **beaucoup plus dynamique**   English meaning: *much*
que l'autre.

– before the adverb **trop**:

L'autre est **beaucoup trop**   English meaning: *much, far*
monotone.

Bien is used:

– with verbs:

Elle a **bien mangé**.   English meaning: *a lot*

– before adjectives:

Nous sommes **bien contents**.   English meaning: *very*

– before adverbs:

Elle va **bien souvent** en France.   English meaning: *quite, very*

– before comparatives with **plus**, **meilleur**, **pire**, and **davantage**:

La valise est **bien plus** lourde
que la mienne.
Cette bière est **bien meilleure**.   English meaning: *much*
Ce vin est **bien pire** que l'autre.
Il boit **bien davantage** que
son amie.

> **Tout** can serve as a determiner and a pronoun, as well as an adverb (see pp. 35–60)

Tout is used to intensify adjectives. It agrees with the adjective only before feminine adjectives that begin with a consonant.

Il est **tout** seul.   Elle est **toute** seule.
Ils sont **tout** seuls.   Elles sont **toutes** seules.

If feminine adjectives begin with a vowel or with h, **tout** is invariable, as adverbs usually are.

Il est **tout** heureux.   Elle est **tout** heureuse.
Ils sont **tout** heureux.   Elles sont **tout** heureuses.

1. Fill in the blanks with the missing forms of the adverbs. *
M. = Michel; S = Sabine

a) M. Tu veux ____vraiment____ acheter une nouvelle voiture ?

b) S. _____ . J'ai _____ demandé à mes

parents. Ils vont me prêter _____ de l'argent pour

pouvoir acheter cette voiture _____ économe en

essence.

c) M. Ecoute-moi _____ . Je ne veux pas que tu roules trop

_____ avec cette nouvelle voiture.

d) S. _____ , je ne te comprends pas. Je n'ai pas envie de

conduire _____ avec ma nouvelle voiture.

e) M. Je sais. Et je sais aussi que tu as travaillé _____ pour

avoir de l'argent. Et en plus, tu as acheté _____. Ça

ne va pas _____ améliorer la situation économique

de notre pays. Tu vas voir, cette discussion va tourner

_____ . Maintenant, je suis _____

touché. Je veux t'expliquer plus _____ la situation :

Il vaut _____ que je te quitte.

a) ~~vrai~~

b) absolu – gentil –
   généreux –
   extrême

c) bon – rapide

d) franc – lent

e) dur – français –
   terrible - mauvais
   – profond – précis
   – meilleur

2. Form adverbs based on the adjectives below. *

a) heureux ____heureusement_____

b) énorme _____

c) profond _____

d) suffisant _____

e) bon _____

f) gentil _____

g) vrai _____

h) poli _____

i) complet _____

j) rare _____

Adverbs

k)   bref   _____

l)   lent   _____

m)   absolu   _____

n)   extrême   _____

o)   courageux   _____

p)   conforme   _____

q)   précis   _____

3. Decide whether an adjective or an adverb is needed to fill in the blanks below. **

a) heureux

b) récent

c) énorme

d) complet

e) meilleur

f) mauvais

g) bon

h) bon

a)   Yvette est une fille _____heureuse_____ .

_____ j'ai pensé à l'anniversaire de ma femme.

b)   Ils ont construit leur maison _____ .

La zone piétonne de notre ville est _____ .

c)   Cet avion fait un bruit _____ .

Oui, tu as raison, il fait _____ de bruit.

d)   Tu fais ton gâteau avec de la farine _____ ?

Oui, mais j'ai _____ oublié d'en acheter.

e)   Je comprends _____ l'italien que l'espagnol.

Mon idée est _____ que celle de Pascal.

f)   Avec ce brouillard, on voit _____ .

C'est une _____ période pour partir en vacances.

g)   Tu vas _____ ?

Oui. Et on a vraiment _____ mangé.

h)   Ça sent _____ chez toi.

Tu as _____ cuisiné.

Numbers and Telling Time

Cardinal Numbers

0	zéro	18	dix-huit	80	quatre-ving**t**s
1	**un, une**	19	dix-neuf	81	quatre-ving**t-un** / **une**
2	deux	20	ving**t**	82	quatre-ving**t**-deux
3	trois	21	ving**t et** un / une	90	quatre-ving**t**-dix
4	quatre	22	ving**t**-deux	91	quatre-ving**t-onze**
5	cinq	23	ving**t**-trois	100	cent
6	six	30	trente	101	cent **un** / **une**
7	sept	31	trente **et** un / une	102	cent deux
8	huit	40	quarante	110	cent dix
9	neuf	41	quarante **et** un / une	180	cent quatre-ving**t**s
10	dix	50	cinquante	200	deux cent**s**
11	onze	51	cinquante **et** un / une	201	deux cent **un** / **une**
12	douze	60	soixante	1 000	mille
13	treize	61	soixante et un / une	1 001	mille **un** / **une**
14	quatorze	70	soixante-**dix**	2 000	deux mill**e**
15	quinze	71	soixante **et** onze	1 000 000	un million
16	seize	72	soixante-douze	2 000 000	deux million**s**
17	dix-sept	73	soixante-treize	1 000 000 000	un milliard

> **!** Pay special attention to the forms of the numbers from 70 to 99!

As numbers, **un** and **une** agree in gender with the noun to which they refer. But if **un** / **une** belongs to a number that follows the noun it refers to, then **un** is always used.

> Tu veux manger combien de bananes ? **Une** ou deux ? – Deux.
> Ce livre contient soixante et **une** pages.
> Mes élèves, ouvrez vos livres à la page soixante et **un**.

With 21, 31, 41, 51, 61, and 71, there is an **et** between the tens and ones.

vingt **et** un	cinquante **et** un
trente **et** un	soixante **et** un
quarante **et** un	soixante **et** onze

After **quatre-vingt**, **cent**, and **mille**, the ones follow directly, without **et**.

quatre-vingt-**un**	cent **un**
	mille **un**

Cardinal Numbers

With the remaining numbers, the ones are attached with a hyphen.

> vingt-deux   quatre-vingt-un
> trente-neuf   quatre-vingt-onze
> soixante-dix-neuf   quatre-vingt-dix-neuf

Numbers that are connected with **cent**, **mille**, **million**, or **milliard** are not hyphenated.

> cent cinquante   trois millions cinq cent mille
> deux mille

Quatre-vingts is spelled with an **-s**, but **vingt** is spelled without an **-s**. If **quatre-vingts** is followed by another number, the **-s** is omitted.

> Ma grand-mère a quatre-vingts ans. Elle s'est mariée à vingt ans.
> Mon grand-père est mort à quatre-vingt-deux ans.

Cent adds an **-s** in the plural only if no other number follows.

> Je voudrais **deux cents** grammes de gruyère râpé et **deux cent cinquante** grammes de parmesan.

Mille is invariable.

> Il me faut aller à la banque pour retirer **deux mille** euros.

Million and **milliard** are variable. A **de** is used after **million** or **milliard** only if no other number follows.

> Cette maison a coûté **deux millions d'**euros.
> Et la maison en Espagne vaut **trois millions cinq cent mille euros**.
> En tout, je possède environs deux **milliards d'**euros.

> **septante** (= 70)
> **nonante** (= 90)
> **huitante** (= 80)

In Belgium and French-speaking Switzerland, **septante** and **nonante** are used officially. **Huitante** is an unofficial regional variant; it appears only in French-speaking Switzerland.

> The first variant of the date, "l'an mille neuf cent quatre-vingts," is preferred.

There are two ways of reading year dates.

> En l'an **mille neuf cent quatre-vingts**...
> En **dix-neuf cent quatre-vingts**...

Ordinal Numbers

1er	le premier	12^e	le/la douzième
1ère	la première	13^e	le/la treizième
2^e	le deuxième	14^e	le/la quatorzième
2^e	la deuxième	15^e	le/la quinzième
2nd	le second	16^e	le/la seizième
2nde	la seconde	17e	le/la dix-septième
3^e	le/la troisième	18e	le/la dix-huitième
4^e	le/la quatrième	19^e	le/la dix-neuvième
5^e	le/la cinquième	20^e	le/la vingtième
6^e	le/la sixième	21^e	le/la vingt et unième
7e	le/la septième	22^e	le/la vingt-deuxième
8e	le/la huitième	31^e	le/la trentième
9^e	le/la neuvième	80^e	le/la quatre-vingtième
10^e	le/la dixième	100^e	le/la centième
11^e	le/la onzième	1000^e	le/la millième

Premier and **second** cannot be linked with other numbers. Instead, use **unième** and **deuxième**.

▶ On dates, see p. 188

vingt et un	▶ le/la vingt et **unième**
cent un	▶ le/la cent **unième**
mille un	▶ le/la mille **unième**

Deuxième and **second(e)** are rendered in English as "the second," and they sometimes are interchangeable. **Second(e)** is more common when there are only "two things."

Overall, **deuxième** is more common than **second(e)**.

> J'aime surtout le **deuxième** chapitre de ce livre.
> La **Seconde** Guerre mondiale était cruelle.
> Comme mon mari est au chômage, j'achète des articles de **second** choix.

With names of rulers, the ordinal number is used only for the "First," otherwise, the cardinal number is used.

> Napoléon Ier (say: premier), Napoléon III (say: trois)
> Elisabeth Ière (say: première)

"Every second, third, ..." corresponds in French to the construction **un / une** + noun + cardinal number.

> J'ai lu **un** livre **sur** deux.
> **Une** maison **sur** cinq date du 18e siècle.

Fractions

> J'ai mangé un quart de ce gâteau.

I've eaten one fourth of this cake.

With the exception of **un demi**, **un tiers**, and **un quart**, fractional numbers are the same as the ordinal numbers.

1/2	un demi
1/3	un tiers
1/4	un quart
1/10	un dixième.
3/4	trois quarts

> **!** If **demi** is placed before the noun (with a hyphen), it is invariable.

Je voudrais **une demi-bouteille** de vin blanc.
I'd like a half bottle of white wine. (small bottle)

Normalement, il boit la **moitié d'une bouteille** de vin blanc.
Normally he drinks half a bottle of white wine. (half of a whole bottle)

Mais hier, il a bu **une bouteille et demie** de vin blanc.
But yesterday he drank one and a half bottles of white wine.

Collective Numbers

> Je voudrais une douzaine d'escargots.

I'd like a dozen snails.

If you want to say that a number amounts to approximately 10, 15, 20, 30, 40, 50, 60, or 100, attach the ending **-aine** to the cardinal number.

une **quinzaine** de jours
une **dizaine** d'amis
une **vingtaine** d'années
une **trentaine** d'invités

"Approximately a thousand" is translated as **un millier**.

Au spectacle, il y avait **un millier** de personnes.

For other numbers, use a circumlocution with **environ** + cardinal number.

environ soixante-dix   *around seventy*
environ quatre-vingts   *around eighty*

"A dozen" (that is, exactly 12) is **une douzaine** in French.

une douzaine d'escargots
une douzaine de serviettes

Telling Time

Quelle heure est-il ?

Vous avez quelle heure ?

What time is it?

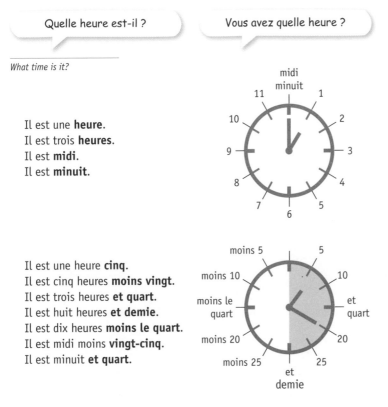

Il est une **heure**.
Il est trois **heures**.
Il est **midi**.
Il est **minuit**.

Il est une heure **cinq**.
Il est cinq heures **moins vingt**.
Il est trois heures **et quart**.
Il est huit heures **et demie**.
Il est dix heures **moins le quart**.
Il est midi moins **vingt-cinq**.
Il est minuit **et quart**.

Official statements of time (at the train station, on the radio, etc.) use the twenty-four-hour clock.

Il est **deux heures trente-cinq**.
Il est **quinze heures cinquante-huit**.
Il est **zéro heure quinze**.

Giving the Date

On est le combien aujourd'hui ?

① On est le premier avril.

Quand est-ce qu'il arrive ?

② Il arrive le quinze mars.

1. What is today's date? – It's the first of April.
2. When is he coming? – He's coming on March 15.

In giving the date, the ordinal number is used to refer only to the first day of the month.

> Je reviendrai le **premier** novembre.
> Il est né le **premier** avril.

From the second through the thirty-first, the cardinal numbers are used.

> Les vacances commencent le **cinq** juillet.
> Cette lettre date **du quatorze** janvier.

▶ On the use of the article in referring to the time of day, the day of the week, and the date, see p. 23

Unlike English, French always uses the definite article without a preposition.

> Il est né **le** neuf décembre.
> Aujourd'hui, nous sommes **le** cinq septembre.

To express a span of time, use the phrase **du ... jusqu'au**.

> Je serai en vacances **du** treize mai **jusqu'au** trois juin.
> *I'll be on vacation **from** May 13 **until** June 3.*

> Il était malade **du** vingt-huit novembre **jusqu'au** premier décembre.
> *He was ill **from** November 28 **until** December 1.*

The definite article is used with the days of the week

– when something occurs <u>habitually</u>:

> **Le** lundi, je dois me lever à six heures. *(every Monday, on Mondays)*
> **Le** dimanche, ma grand-mère va à l'eglise. *(every Sunday, on Sundays)*

– and when a date follows:

> Aujourd'hui, nous sommes **le** jeudi 10 mai.
> Je suis revenu **le** samedi 20 septembre.

1. Rewrite the following dates in the French manner. Spell out the names of the months. *

a) April 20, 2005   _____20 avril 2005_____

b) September 1, 1939   _____

c) November 11, 1918   _____

d) January 1, 2000   _____

2. Write out the following official times, using words rather than numbers. *

a) 3 h 15   _____trois heures quinze_____

b) 15 h 18   _____

c) 20 h 15   _____

d) 0 h 20   _____

e) 8 h 30   _____

f) 12 h 45   _____

g) 16 h 00   _____

h) 2 h 50   _____

3. How do you say these times in French? Write out these times, expressed in colloquial French. *

a) 3 h 15   _____trois heures quinze_____

b) 5 h 30   _____

c) 18 h 45   _____

d) 22 h 20   _____

e) 12 h 00   _____

f) 24 h 00   _____

g) 5 h 50   _____

h) 7 h 55   _____

i) 17 h 30   _____

j) 6 h 30   _____

k) 15 h 15   _____

Numbers and Telling Time

l) 5 h 45 _____

m) 2 h 05 _____

n) 8 h 00 _____

o) 3 h 30 _____

4. A teacher is talking to his class. Translate the material in **bold** into French. Spell out the numbers. **

a) Open your book to **page 31.**

   page trente et un _____

b) Now do problem **21.**

   _____

c) How much is **1/2 × 1/4** ?

   _____

d) Exactly! It's **1/8.**

   _____

e) **Approximately 15** problems are difficult.

   _____

f) And on **every fifth problem**, you really have to think.

   _____

g) What is **200** times **250?**

   _____

h) Exactly! It's **50,000.**

   _____

i) Multiply **80** by **82.**

   _____

j) Exactly! It's **8,560.**

   _____

Prepositions

In French, the meaning of prepositions depends heavily on the following nouns.

Always memorize French prepositions along with examples because their meaning is highly dependent on context.

The Prepositions of Place *à, dans, en*

à

> J'habite à Paris.

I live in Paris.

The preposition **à** is used to indicate place, in answer to the questions "Where?" or "Where to?". It also is used with most masculine names of countries and with names of islands if not accompanied by an article. Examples: le Portugal, le Luxembourg, le Danemark, le Royaume-Uni, les Etats-Unis, les Pays-Bas, le Maroc, le Japon, Malte, Jersey, Chypre, Madagascar, Cuba.

English equivalent	Question	Example
in	where?	Le groupe de voyage est **à Paris** aujourd'hui.
to	where to?	Les Dupont vont **au musée**.
to	where to?	L'été prochain, nous allons **au Portugal** ou **aux Etats-Unis**.

Note: Je vais **à la** banque. – *I'm going to the bank*. Je vais **dans une** banque. – *I'm going to a bank*.

191

dans

> J'habite dans un grand appartement.

I live in a large apartment.

Whereas **à** indicates place only in a general way, **dans** is used with concrete expressions of place, which often contain the indefinite article **un** or **une**. In addition, **dans** is used with the names of most of the French **départements**.

but: Dimanche, on va **au** musée.

Saint-Denis se trouve **au nord** de Paris. – *north of*; Montmartre se trouve **dans le nord de** Paris. – *in the north of*

English equivalent	Question	Example
to	where to?	Dimanche, on va **dans un musée** d'art moderne.
in	where?	J'ai passé un an **dans le Nord-Pas-de-Calais.**
to	where to?	L'année prochaine, je vais **dans le Finistère.**
in	where?	Les enfants jouent **dans la rue.**

en

Pay special attention to the construction **dans la rue.**

> Nous avons passé les vacances en Italie.

We spent our vacation in Italy.

The preposition **en** is used – generally without an article – with feminine names of countries, with the names of French provinces, and in certain expressions.

English equivalent	Question	Example
to	where to?	Nous allons souvent **en Allemagne.**
in	where?	Nous avons des amis **en Provence.**
to	where to?	Samedi prochain, on va **en ville.**
		En route, nous avons vu beaucoup d'animaux.

en route – *on the way, in transit*

Other Prepositions of Place

à côté de	Le cinéma est **à côté du théâtre**. *(next to)*
au-dessous de	**Au-dessous de chez-moi**, il y a un restaurant chinois. *(below, under)*
au-dessus de	J'habite **au-dessus d'un salon de coiffure**. *(above, over)*
à droite de	**A droite de l'Hôtel de Ville**, il y a une boulangerie. *(to the right of)*
au milieu de	La fontaine se trouve **au milieu de la place**. *(in the middle of)*
au nord de	Amiens est **au nord de Paris**. *(north of)*
à travers	Ils marchent **à travers le désert**. *(through, across)*
autour de	**Autour de la fontaine**, il y a des chaises. *(around)*
chez	Lundi prochain, je vais **chez le dentiste**. *(to)* On va passer nos vacances **chez nos parents**. *(with, in the home of)*
contre	Elle pousse le lit **contre le mur**. *(against)*
de	Il vient **de Paris**. *(from)*
derrière	Le livre est tombé **derrière la bibliothèque**. *(behind)*
devant	Il a posé le paquet **devant la porte**. *(in front of)*
en face de	Notre hôtel est **en face de l'église**. *(opposite, across from)*
entre	La principauté d'Andorre se trouve **entre la France et l'Espagne**. *(between)*
jusque	Il y a un bouchon **jusqu'à l'aéroport**. *(all the way to)*

Other Prepositions of Place

le long de	On va faire une promenade **le long du fleuve** ? *(along)*
loin de	La gare est **loin du centre-ville**. *(far from)*
par	Pour aller à Marseille, nous passons **par Lyon**. *(through)*
parmi	**Parmi nos amis**, il y a beaucoup de Français. *(among)*
pour	Les voyageurs **pour Jersey** sont priés de prendre le bateau. *(to, for)*
près de	Le théâtre est **près de la mairie**. *(close to, near)*
sous	Le chien est **sous la table**. *(under)*
sur	Mettez les verres **sur la table**. *(on)* Les chambres donnent **sur le jardin**. *(open onto, have a view of)* St. Louis est située **sur le Mississippi**. *(on)*
vers	Cette année, beaucoup de Français partent **vers la Bretagne**. *(to, in the direction of)*

Prepositions of Time

Je le connais depuis cinq ans.

I've known him for five years.

A demain ! –
Until tomorrow!
A tout à l'heure ! –
See you soon!
A la prochaine ! –
Until next time!

à	**A trois heures**, je suis à la gare. *(at)* La famille Dupont est partie **à midi**. *(at)* Nous allons faire du ski **au printemps** mais pas en hiver. *(in)*
au mois de	Cette année, nous allons en vacances **au mois d'août**. *(in August*; instead of **en août***)*
à partir de	**A partir d'aujourd'hui**, je ne fume plus. *(from today on, starting today*; beginning in the present or future*)*

après	Nous avons beaucoup travaillé **après les vacances**. *(after)*
avant	Nos amis vont venir **avant dix heures**. *(before)*
dans	**Dans une semaine**, je vais à Paris. *(in, ...from now)* *But:* Je suis allé à Paris en une heure. *(in, within)*
de... à	Je travaille de **lundi à samedi**, **du matin au soir**. *(from ... to)*
depuis	On passe nos vacances en France **depuis des années**. *(for)* **Depuis ce jour-là**, il ne fume plus. *(from ... on)*
dès	Il savait lire **dès l'âge de 5 ans**. *(from, since)*
en	On va à la piscine **en été**, **en automne**, **en hiver** mais pas au printemps. *(in)* Ma fille est née **en 1997**. *(in)* J'ai préparé ce repas **en deux heures**. *(in, in the space of)*
entre... et	Nous passerons chez vous **entre huit et neuf heures.** *(between ... and)*
il y a	J'ai été à Bruxelles **il y a deux mois**. *(ago)*
jusque	J'ai travaillé **jusqu'à trois heures** du matin. *(until)*
pendant	**Pendant les vacances**, on ne travaille pas. *(during)*
pour	Elle est partie au Canada **pour six mois**. *(for)*
vers	Elle est morte **vers trois heures** de l'après-midi. *(at, toward)*

Modal Prepositions

Tu es arrivé en voiture ?

Non, je suis venu à bicyclette.

Did you come by car? – No, I came on my bike.

à

A distinction is made between movement <u>in</u> a means of transportation (**en** voiture) and <u>on</u> a means of transportation (**à** bicyclette).

Au supermarché, il achète encore **six tasses à café**.	*coffee cups* (purpose)
On peut laver ce pull **à la machine** ?	*with, in* (manner)
Il va à Strasbourg **à bicyclette**.	*by, on* (**on** a means of transportation)
Le jambon est **à dix euros** le kilo.	*costs … per kilo* (prices)
Metz est **à trois cents kilomètres** de Paris.	*located … from* (statements of distance)

avec

Coupe la viande **avec ton couteau**.   *with* (tool or means)

de

Tu prends encore une tasse **de thé** ?	*a cup of tea* (content, quantity)
Je lui fais signe **de la main**.	*by* (part of the body)
Les gens sont morts **de faim**.	*of* (cause)
Elle porte une jupe **de soie**.	*of* (material)

en

Les Dupont arrivent **en avion**.	*by* (in a means of transportation)
J'ai acheté un pull **en laine**.	*of* (material)

par

J'ai envoyé un livre **par la poste**.	*by* (means)
J'ai appris la nouvelle **par mon père**.	*through* (agent)
Elle est restée chez les voisins **par pitié**.	*out of* (cause, motive)
Ils vont au restaurant deux fois **par semaine**.	
Le buffet coûte 18 euros **par personne**.	*per* (distribution)

pour

Il a acheté une maison **pour sa femme**.	*for* (purpose)
Elle est partie **pour une semaine**.	*for* (duration)
Il a acheté cette voiture **pour quinze mille euros**.	*for* (price)

sur

Un allemand **sur trois** connaît la France.	*out of* (distribution)
Elle va **sur ses cinquante ans**.	*nearly* (age)

Practice and Application

1. Fill in the blanks, using the prepositions **à**, **dans**, **en**, plus the definite or indefinite article where called for. *

_au_	restaurant
_____	Paris
_____	Portugal
_____	sud de la France
_____	Grenoble
_____	Bas-Rhin
_____	Italie
_____	Cuba
_____	Pays-Bas
_____	pied
_____	cinéma
_____	voiture
_____	Suisse
_____	montagne
_____	Japon
_____	Bourgogne
_____	Var
_____	train
_____	moto

aller

2. Supply the missing prepositions of place and, where needed, the missing articles. *

le, l', les,
à, au,
en, dans,
chez, de

a) La piscine est ___à___ côté _____ gare.

b) Orléans est _____ sud _____ Paris.

c) Pour demain, j'ai pris un rendez-vous _____ médecin.

d) La famille Dupont vient _____ Brest.

e) Dimanche, j'irai _____ campagne.

f) Nous irons _____ Alpes pour faire du ski.

g) Michel est resté _____ Washington _____ Etats-Unis.

3. Two people, Barbara (B.) and Michel (M.), are talking about their travel experiences. Fill in the correct prepositions and/or articles.

B. : L'an dernier, j'ai passé mes vacances __au__ Portugal. Les Portugais sont des gens très gentils. Mais il y avait un problème : Je ne parle pas le portugais.

M. : Je connais ça. Il y a deux ans, on a visité Copenhague. Personne de ma famille ne parle ___ danois. Et ___ Danemark, ce n'est pas évident qu'on y parle ___ français.

B. : De toute façon, moi je préfère les pays francophones.

M. : En Europe, dans quels états est-ce qu'on parle le français comme langue officielle ?

B. : C'est ___ France, ___ Belgique, ___ Luxembourg et ___ Suisse. ___ Monaco, il y a deux langues officielles : ___ italien et ___ français. Et ___ Italie, ___ val d'Aoste, ___ français est officiellement une langue régionale.

M. : En dehors de l'Europe, le français joue un rôle important ?

B. : Oui, ___ Canada, ___ français est la deuxième langue après l'anglais. Et ___ Québec, ___ français est l'unique langue officielle. Dans une vingtaine de pays d'Afrique, par exemple ___ République Centrafricaine ou ___ Madagascar, ___ français est langue officielle, souvent à côté d'autres. ___ Liban, ___ Algérie, ___ Maroc et ___ Tunisie ___ français est langue d'enseignement. ___ ___ départements et territoires d'outre mer, qui font partie de la République française, ___ Guadeloupe, ___ Martinique où ___ Saint-Pierre-et-Miquelon, le français est bien sûr langue officielle.

> le Canada,
> le Québec,
> la République Centrafricaine,
> Madagascar,
> l'Algérie,
> le Maroc,
> la Tunisie,
> la Guadeloupe,
> la Martinique,
> Saint-Pierre-et-Miquelon

> The "départements et territoires d'outre mer" often are referred to as "les DOM – TOM."

Prepositions

4. Fill in the missing prepositions of time. In some sentences, there are several possibilities! **

a) Pascal est né ___en___ 1976.

b) _____ juin et juillet, nous serons en vacances.

c) Nous partirons _____ deux heures du matin.

d) Michèle est venue _____ trois heures.

e) Pascal est parti, il va revenir _____ quinze jours.

f) Annick est partie _____ six mois.

g) Il y avait une grande fête à Orléans _____ trois mois.

h) Aujourd'hui, je travaille seulement _____ deux heures.

5. Which prepositions are missing in these sentences?

a) Cet appartement n'appartient pas __à__ Annick mais ____ Pascal.

b) _____ quinze jours, Pascal va venir _____ avion.

c) Il nous a envoyé une lettre _____ avion.

d) Voilà les tasses _____ café et les tasses _____ thé.

e) Je suis fatiguée. Tu me donnes une tasse _____ café ?

f) Je me suis acheté douze verres _____ cristal _____ 200 euros.

g) _____ midi, j'ai rencontré une vieille amie _____ la rue.

h) Il connaît la grammaire française _____ A _____ Z.

Conjunctions

Conjunctions are used to connect words, phrases, clauses, or sentences. It is important to know that in French, many conjunctions must be followed by the **subjunctive** or the **conditional**.

▶ On the subjunctive, see the section beginning on p. 118

▶ On the conditional, see the section beginning on p. 113

Subjunctive	Conditional	No special form required
avant que	au cas où	jusqu'au moment où
jusqu'à ce que	dans le cas où	avant le moment où
en attendant que	pour le cas où	depuis que
pour que	dans l'hypothèse où	quand
afin que		lorsque
de peur que		pendant que
de crainte que		tandis que
de sorte que		en même temps que
de façon que		chaque fois que
de manière que		tant que
sans que		aussi longtemps que
bien que		après que
quoique		dès que
malgré que		aussitôt que
à condition que		une fois que
pourvu que		comme
à supposer que		parce que
à moins que		puisque
		du fait que
		étant donné que
		vu que
		de sorte que
		de façon que
		de manière que

en attendant que – *until*
jusqu'à ce que – *until*
depuis que – *since*
lorsque (in the past) – *when*
lorsque (in the future) – *when, if*
tandis que – *while, whereas*
dès que – *as soon as*
aussitôt que – *as soon as*
une fois que – *once*

Use

The subjunctive is <u>always</u> used :

bien que, quoique,
malgré que – *although*

Bien qu'il n'ait pas de chance dans la vie, il a gagné le gros lot.
Quoique je sois jeune, j'ai déjà beaucoup travaillé.
Malgré qu'elle soit très occupée, elle va régulièrement au cinéma.

– after the expressions of qualification or reservation **bien que**, **quoique**, and **malgré que**.

Rappelle-moi **avant que** tu partes.
Les gens sont descendus dans la rue **jusqu'à ce que** les responsables politiques démissionnent.

– after the conjunctions **avant que**, **en attendant que** and **jusqu'à ce que, sans que**.

pour que, afin que –
so that
de peur que –
for fear that
de crainte que–
for fear that
à condition que –
on condition that,
provided that
pourvu que –
provided that
à supposer que –
assuming that
à moins que – *unless*

Elle a économisé énormément d'argent **pour que** sa famille puisse partir en vacances.
Recule la voiture **afin que** je puisse rentrer au garage.

– after the expressions of purpose **pour que**, **afin que**, **de peur que**, and **de crainte que**.

Tu pourras sortir ce soir **à condition que** tu fasses tes devoirs demain.
Nous irons faire un tour **à moins qu'**il fasse mauvais temps.

– after **à condition que**, **pourvu que**, **à supposer que**, and **à moins que**.

<u>No subjunctive</u> is used:

Cet après-midi, nous irons à la plage. Nous resterons **jusqu'au moment où** la nuit tombera.

– after **avant le moment où** and **jusqu'au moment où**.

Depuis qu'il avait reçu notre lettre, il ne nous parlait plus.

– after **depuis que** – here the present tense or one of the past tenses is used.

Comme je ne me sens pas bien, je ne travaille pas aujourd'hui.
Il ne travaille pas aujourd'hui **parce qu'**il ne se sent pas bien.
Puisque il va en vacances, il a prêté sa maison à des amis.

– after the expressions of substantiation **comme**, **parce que**, **puisque**, **du fait que**, **étant donné que**, and **vu que**. Here the appropriate tense is used.

comme (at the beginning of a sentence) –
since, as
puisque – *since, because, as*
du fait que –
by the fact that
étant donné que –
in light of the fact that
vu que – *seeing that*

Au cas où mes parents viendraient, j'ai laissé la clé sous le paillasson.
Dans l'hypothèse où je ne trouverais pas de travail, je me suis inscrit à l'université.

After the expressions of condition **au cas où**, **pour le cas où**, and **dans l'hypothèse où**, the conditional is used, rather than the subjunctive.

au cas où – *in case*
dans l'hypothèse où –
on the assumption that

Je vous ai fait les bagages **de façon que** vous pouvez partir en vacanes.
Il a préparé le dîner **de (telle) manière** que sa femme était très contente.
Il faut nettoyer l'appartement **de sorte que** les amis puissent venir.

de sorte, de façon, de manière que – *so that* (actual or intended result)

The subjunctive is not used after the expressions of consequence **de sorte que**, **de façon que**, and **de manière que**. However, if the consequence is not actual, but merely intended, the subjunctive is used here as well.

Practice and Application

1. Insert the appropriate verb forms for the following conjunctions of time. ***

faire une drôle de tête – *to make a face*
changer – *to change*

a) Pendant que tu __choisis__ un jeans, je vais regarder les T-shirts. (choisir)

b) Avant que tu _____ , il faut bien réfléchir. (choisir)

c) Dès que tu _____ ton jeans, on quittera le magasin. (payer)

d) Une fois qu'on _____ le magasin, on ira chez tes parents. (quitter)

e) On y restera jusqu'à ce que ton frère _____ . (venir)

f) Depuis qu'il _____ en Belgique, il a vraiment changé. (habiter)

g) Chaque fois qu'il était chez tes parents, il _____ une drôle de tête. (faire)

h) Et la dernière fois, lorsque j' _____ en parler, il _____ qu'il n'y avait rien. (vouloir / répondre)

2. With the following conjunctions of condition, decide whether the subjunctive or the conditional is required. ***

a) Nous irons à la piscine à condition qu'il ne __pleuve__ pas. (pleuvoir)

b) Au cas où la piscine _____ , on ira au restaurant. (être fermé)

c) A moins qu'il y _____ trop de gens. Dans ce cas nous rentrerions dîner à la maison. (avoir)

d) Dans le cas où le réfrigérateur _____ vide, on appellera le pizza-service. (être)

e) En attendant que le pizza-service _____ , nous jouerons aux cartes. (venir)

3. Translate the following sentences into French, using the conjunctions in parentheses. ***

a) Write me before you come. (avant que)

   Appelle-moi avant que je parte au bureau.

b) As soon as you've arrived, we'll go out to eat. (dès que)

c) Because you're a vegetarian, we won't eat any meat. (puisque)

d) While I write to you, I'm watching a film. (pendant que)

e) I've saved a lot of money so that we can go to a nice restaurant.
   (pour que)

The Declarative Sentence and the Interrogative Sentence

The Declarative Sentence

1. M. Dutour montre sa nouvelle voiture à son collègue.

---

1. *Monsieur Dutour is showing the new car to his colleague.*

A declarative sentence has the following word order:

Subject	Verb	Direct Object	à Object
M. Dutour	montre	sa nouvelle voiture	à son collègue.

In French, the direct object precedes the **à** object. In English, the indirect object may also come first: *Monsieur Dutour is showing his colleague the new car.*

In French, the subject is emphasized by the expression **C'est ... qui ....** English can use equivalent constructions, in addition to intonation, for emphasis.

> **C'est M. Dutour qui** a acheté une nouvelle voiture.
> *It's <u>Monsieur Dutour</u> who bought a new car. / <u>Monsieur Dutour</u> is the one who bought a new car.*

If you want to emphasize the direct object or the **à** object, you can introduce that element with **C'est ... que**. Then normal word order follows: subject, verb, (other) object.

> **C'est à son collègue que** M. Dutour montre sa nouvelle voiture.
> *It's <u>to his colleague</u> that Monsieur Dutour is showing his new car.*

> **C'est sa nouvelle voiture que** M. Dutour montre à son collègue.
> *It's <u>the new car</u> that Monsieur Dutour is showing to his colleague.*

> ! A simple rearrangement of the parts of speech is not sufficient to lend emphasis in French.

Adverbs of time or place generally can be placed first or last in the sentence. At the beginning of a sentence, a statement of place or time is followed by a comma. It does not affect normal word order.

A 6 h 30, je me lève.
At 6:30 I get up.

Je me lève **à 6 h 30**.
I get up at 6:30.

Sur le parking, M. Dutour montre sa nouvelle voiture à son collègue.
In the parking lot, Monsieur Dutour is showing his new car to his colleague.

If expressions of both time and place occur in a sentence, usually the expression of time is placed first, and the statement of place is in the final position.

Aujourd'hui, elle est allée **à Paris**.
Today she went to Paris.

Indefinite adverbs of place, time, or manner that do not end in **-ment** are used with:

▶ On the placement of adverbs ending in **–ment**; see p. 176

– simple tenses (such as the present, imperfect, simple future), after the verb:

Elle part **déjà**.
Il mangeait **beaucoup**.
Elle comprend **bien**.

– compound tenses, after **avoir** or **être** and before the past participle:

Elle est **déjà** partie.
Il a **beaucoup** mangé.
Elle a **bien** compris.

– sentences with an infinitive, before the infinitive:

Elle va **bientôt** partir.
Il veut **toujours** avoir raison.

The Interrogative Sentence

Tu vas bien? – Oui.

Decision Question (yes-or-no question)

The person addressed answers a decision question with **oui**, **non**, or **si**.

Tu vas bien ? positive question	**– Oui.** – positive answer
Tu as faim ? positive question	**– Non.** – negative answer
Tu ne vas pas à Paris ? negative question	**– Si.** – positive answer
Tu n'es pas d'accord ? negative question	**– Non.** – negative answer

There are four possible ways of forming a decision question.

1. Intonation question

In an intonation question, the word order of the declarative sentence is retained. This type occurs primarily in spoken French.

Ça va **?**
Michel est déjà parti **?**
Toi aussi, tu vas à Paris **?**

2. *Est-ce que* question

In an **est-ce que** question, you simply place **est-ce que** before a normal declarative sentence. Questions with **est-ce que** occur in both spoken and written French.

Est-ce que tu vas bien ?
Est-ce que Michel est déjà parti ?
Est-ce que tu vas à Paris ?

3. Inversion question

In an inversion question, the subject pronoun is linked to the verb with a hyphen.

> **Partez-vous** souvent en vacances ?
> Et votre femme ? **Ne prend-elle** pas la voiture ?
> Et votre oncle ? **Parle-t-il** bien le français ?

> If the third person singular (il, elle, on) ends in **-e** or **-a**, then a **-t-** is inserted before the subject pronoun. !

In a negated sentence, **ne** precedes the conjugated verb, and **pas** follows the subject pronoun. Inversion questions are typical of literary French.

N'a-t-il pas fait de progrès ?

The order of noun and verb cannot simply be reversed to form an interrogative sentence. Instead, French places the subject first in the sentence, and in addition the appropriate subject pronoun is attached with a hyphen, as is usual in inversion questions.

Vos enfants partent-ils en vacances ?
Votre femme ne **prend-elle** pas la voiture ?
Votre oncle parle-t-il bien le français ?

Probe Question (question with an interrogative word)

> A question such as "Partent vos enfants?" is not possible in French. !

The person addressed does not answer a probe question with **oui**, **non**, or **si** but with another word or an entire sentence.

Quand est-ce que tu pars à Paris ? – **Demain.**
Qu'est-ce que tu as fait à Paris ? – **Tous les soirs, je suis allé au cinéma.**

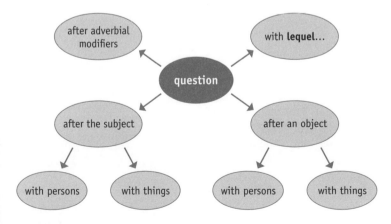

1. Question about the subject

a) with persons: ... *"who?"*

qui est-ce qui... or qui	Qui est-ce qui a pris la voiture ? Qui a pris la voiture ? Michel a pris la voiture.

– in connection with **être**:

Written French	Spoken French
qui est.../qui sont...	c'est qui ...
Qui sont ces gens-là ?	C'est qui, ces gens-là ? – Ce sont des voisins.

b) with things: *"what?"*, *"which?"*

▶ On **quel**, see p. 38

qu'est-ce qui ...	Qu'est-ce qui s'est passé ? Une chose terrible s'est passée.
bei **être: quel...**	Quelle est votre voiture ? Voilà ma voiture.

2. Question about an object

a) with persons: *"whom?"*, *"to whom?"*, *"for whom?"*

– question about the direct object (whom?):

Written French	Spoken French
qui est-ce que, qui + inversion	qui placed after
Qui est-ce que tu as vu ? Qui as-tu vu ?	Tu as vu qui ? J'ai vu Michel.

– question about the **à** object (whom?, to / for whom?)

Written French	Spoken French
à qui est-ce que, à qui + inversion	à qui placed after
A qui est-ce que tu as parlé ? A qui as-tu parlé ?	Tu as parlé à qui ? J'ai parlé à Michel.

– question about the **de** object (of whom?, about whom?)

Written French	Spoken French
de qui est-ce que, **de qui** + inversion	**de qui** placed after
De qui est-ce que tu as parlé ? **De qui as-tu** parlé ?	Tu as parlé **de qui** ? J'ai parlé de Michel.

b) with things: *what?*, *to what?*, *about what?*

– question about the direct object (what?):

Written French	Spoken French
qu'est-ce que, **que** + inversion	**quoi** placed after
Qu'est-ce que tu veux ? **Que veux-tu** ?	Tu veux **quoi** ? Je veux une voiture.

– question about the **à** object (about what?, of what?):

Written French	Spoken French
à quoi est-ce que, **à quoi** + inversion	**à quoi** placed after
A quoi est-ce que tu penses ? **A quoi penses-tu** ?	Tu penses **à quoi** ? Je pense aux vacances.

– question about the **de** object (about what?, with what?, of what?):

Written French	Spoken French
de quoi est-ce que, **de quoi** + inversion	**de quoi** placed after
De quoi est-ce que tu parles ? **De** quoi parles-tu ?	Tu parles **de quoi** ? Je parle d'une fête.

<table>
</table>

With questions about manner (using **comment ...**, for example), cause or motive (**pourquoi ...**), number (**combien ...**), and after other adverbs, in principle the same rules apply as with questions about place or time.

3. Questions about the place, the time, and other adverbial modifiers

– question about the place (where?):

Written French	Spoken French
où est-ce que, où + inversion	**où** placed after
Où est-ce qu'il va ? **Où va-t-il** ?	Il va **où** ? Il va à Paris.

– question about the time (when?):

Written French	Spoken French
quand est-ce que, quand + inversion	**quand** placed after
Quand est-ce qu'il part ? **Quand part-il** ?	Il part **quand** ? Il part à midi.

4. Questions with *lequel* ... (which ?)

Instead of **quel** + noun, you can also use the interrogative determiner **lequel...** This is especially useful if the noun is already known.
Lequel, like **quel**, agrees in number and gender with the noun it refers to.

Je voudrais dix œufs. – **Lesquels** ? – Ceux-ci.
Et un kilo de tomates. – **Lesquelles** ? – Celles-ci.
Et un chou-fleur. – **Lequel** ? – Celui-là.
Et une noix de coco. – **Laquelle** ? – Celle-là.

If **lequel** refers to a noun with a preposition, then this preposition must be placed before the given form. In this case, **à** and **de** and the forms of **lequel** combine to create these contractions: **auquel**, **auxquels**, **auxquelles** and **duquel**, **desquels**, **desquelles**. Other prepositions do not form contractions.

Ce soir, nous sommes invités **chez** nos voisins. – **Chez lesquels** ?
On va faire nos courses **au** supermarché. – **Auquel** ?
Vous me coupez un morceau de fromage ? – **Duquel** ?

1. Fill in the blanks with the missing prepositions. *

a) __Où___ est-ce que vous allez ?   – A Lille.

b) _____ est-ce que vous venez ?   – De Bruxelles.

c) _____ est-ce que vous partez ? – A dix heures du soir.

d) _____ parlez-vous ?   – De Monsieur Dutour.

e) _____ penses-tu ?   – Aux prochaines vacances.

f) _____ écrivez-vous ?   – Au président de la République.

2. Insert **qui est-ce qui**, **qui est-ce que**, **qu'est-ce qui**, or **qu'est-ce que**. **

a) __Qu'est-ce que_____ c'est comme voiture ?

C'est une BMW.

b) _____ écoute de la musique si fort ?

Ce sont nos voisins.

c) _____ on mange ce soir ?

On mange des légumes et des fruits.

d) _____ il cherche ?

Il cherche sa fille.

e) _____ s'est passé ?

Sa fille est partie depuis hier soir.

f) _____ Michel fait toute la journée ?

Il écrit des poèmes.

g) _____ va aider la pauvre voisine ?

Michel va aider la pauvre voisine.

h) _____ se trouve dans le grenier ?

Des tableaux et des meubles se trouvent dans le grenier.   le grenier – *attic, loft*

The Interrogative Sentence

3. Reword these questions with **est-ce que** to create questions using inversion. **

a) Est-ce que vous êtes Française ?

   Etes-vous Française   ?

b). Est-ce qu'il va en France pour faire des études ?

                                             ?

c) Est-ce que vous avez voyagé beaucoup ?

                                             ?

d) Est-ce que vous prenez souvent l'avion ?

                                             ?

e) Est-ce qu'elle n'a pas pris la voiture ?

                                             ?

f) Est-ce que votre femme connaît déjà la nouvelle collection ?

                                             ?

g) Est-ce que votre mari va en ville demain ?

                                             ?

h) Est-ce que le président n'a pas donné une interview ?

                                             ?

4. Ask questions containing **lequel**. **

a) Mes voisins m'énervent. – _Lesquels_ ?

b) En Bourgogne, il y a des villes très agréables. – _____ ?

c) Il parle d'un centre touristique pittoresque. – _____ ?

d) Ma mère est allée chez le médecin. – _____ ?

e) Vous nous mettez trois bières ? – _____ ?

f) On a parlé des poètes français en classe. – _____ ?

g) Tu sais à quel livre je pense souvent ? – _____ ?

h) Tu as déjà répondu à ton amie ? – _____ ?

i) Tu te souviens de ta vieille tante ? – _____ ?

Answers

Nouns (pp. 19–20)

1. b) une nièce; c) un roi;
d) une institutrice;
e) un camarade; f) un criminel;
g) une peintre; h) un duc;
i) une invitée; j) une victime

2. b) the critic, the critique;
c) the party, the part;
d) the stove, the pan;
e) the tour, the tower;
f) the morale, the morals/ethics

3. b) les détails; c) les maux;
d) les bijoux; e) les cours;
f) les yeux; g) les cous;
h) les canaux; i) les bateaux;
j) les gaz; k) les os

4.

Masculine Nouns		Feminine Nouns	
Singular	Plural	Singular	Plural
le monsieur	les messieurs	l'Espagnole	les Espagnoles
l'ouvrier	les ouvriers	la chienne	les chiennes
le Belge	les Belges	l'adolescente	les adolescentes
le secrétaire	les secrétaires	l'actrice	les actrices
le médecin	les médecins	la Belge	les Belges
le romantisme	---	la secrétaire	les secrétaires
le mouchoir	les mouchoirs	la fusée	les fusées
l'ordinateur	les ordinateurs	la baguette	les baguettes
le détail	les détails	la maladie	les maladies
le cheval	les chevaux	la décision	les décisions
le prix	les prix	la perceuse	les perceuses
le nez	les nez	la révision	les révisions
l'œil	les yeux	la différence	les différences
le bal	les bals	la crise	les crises
le soleil	les soleils	la faiblesse	les faiblesses
le bois	les bois	l'image	les images
l'hôtel	les hôtels	la dent	les dents

Articles (pp. 26 – 27)

1. b) une; c) un; d) des; e) un;
   f) des; g) des; h) un; i) une;
   j) un; k) des; l) un
2. b) sont – les;
   c) est – la – la;
   d) sont – les – la;
   e) sont – les – la;
   f) est – l' – la;
   g) sont – les – (no article)
3. b) un – (no article);
   c) de – de;
   d) un – de – un – de;
   e) la;
   f) de;
   g) (no article)
   h) du – la;
   i) une – de – une;
   j) la;
   k) la – du – du – un – des;
   l) les – une – de;
   m) un
4. a) du lait – de lait – de lait
   b) du fromage – de gruyère –
   un peu de fromage – pas de
   fromage – du / un camembert
   c) comme fruits – des pommes –
   des oranges – des kiwis – des
   ananas – les kiwis – pas les
   ananas – combien les oranges
   – un kilo de pommes –
   six kiwis
   d) des fraises – pas de fraises –
   la plupart des gens –
   le supermarché – la plus
   grande partie des fruits
   e) l'addition – un billet de
   20 euros – la monnaie –
   à la prochaine

Demonstrative Determiners (p. 30)

1. b) ce; c) cette; d) ce; e) ces;
   f) ce; g) ce; h) cette; i) cette;
   j) cette; k) ces; l) ce

Possessive Determiners (p. 34)

1. b) son frère; c) sa mère;
   d) son père e) ses enfants;
   f) leur fils; g) leur fille;
   h) leurs enfants

Indefinite Determiners (p. 37)

1. b) tous les kiwis;
   c) elles ont mangé tout
   l'ananas;
   d) elles ont mangé tous les
   spaghetti;
   e) elles ont bu toute la
   limonade;
   f) elles ont mangé toutes les
   bananes
2. b) Un certain Monsieur Gilles
   dit que la musique est très
   importante.
   c) Certains enfants ne disent
   pas la vérité.
   d) Un certain nombre de
   personnes ont disparu.
   e) Il restera un certain temps.
   f) Dans certains pays, les gens
   n'ont pas assez à manger.

Interrogative Determiners (p. 40)

1. b) Quelle; c) Quelles;
   d) Quel / Quels; e) Quelle;
   f) quel; g) quels; h) Quels

Pronouns (pp. 45 – 46)

1. b) Non, je ne l'ai pas vu.
   c) je ne les ai pas
   d) ne les ai pas vues.
   e) je ne l'ai pas vu.
   f) ne l'ai pas vu.
   g) ne l'ai pas vue.
2. b) Je ne l'aime plus.
   c) Il l'admire trop.
   d) Il la trouve sympa.
   e) Il lui téléphone tous les jours.
   f) Elle les lui a demandées.
   g) Il l'attend à la maison.
   h) Elle nous appartient.
   i) Nous l'avons achetée.
   j) Je ne l'accepte plus.
   k) Je vais le quitter.
   l) Je vais les jeter dehors.
   m) Je vais la lui raconter.
   n) Il ne l'a jamais comprise.

Placement of Object and Adverbial Pronouns (pp. 51 – 52)

1. b) Nous y arriverons à 14 heures 25.
   c) J'en ai déjà parlé la semaine dernière.
   d) J'y pense déjà.
   e) Nous allons y monter.
   f) Je peux en acheter deux.
2. b) en; c) en; d) y;
   e) en; f) en; g) y

3. b) Si, je l'ai vu.
   c) Oui, on y va.
   d) Oui, je lui dirai bonjour.
   e) Oui, je vais lui téléphoner prochainement.
   f) Non, je ne pense pas souvent à elle.
   g) Non, elle n'y travaille plus.
   h) Non, il ne s'y intéresse plus.
   i) Non, il n'y travaille plus.
   j) Oui, elle leur appartient toujours.
   k) Non, ils n'en ont pas changé.
   l) Non, ils n'ont pas besoin d'elle.
   m) Si, elle l'a aidée.

Stressed (Disjunctive) Personal Pronouns (p. 54)

1. b) avec lui; c) avec vous;
   d) avec elle; e) avec elles;
   f) avec eux
2. b) Il ne veut pas aller avec lui non plus.
   c) Et Florence ne va pas avec eux non plus.
   d) Et lui, il est d'accord avec elle.
   e) Et elle ne voudrait pas se disputer avec lui.
   f) Tous ne veulent pas aller chez eux.

Demonstrative Pronouns (p. 57)

1. b) celui c) celle-là; d) Celle;
   e) Celles-ci ou celles-là;
   f) celles; g) celle;
   h) Celui-ci – celui-là;
   i) celui; j) celui-ci, celui-là;
   k) Celui-ci

Possessive Pronouns (p. 59)

1. b) le mien;
   c) les miens;
   d) Ce sont les miennes;
   e) ce sont les siens;
   f) Oui, ce sont les siens;
   g) Oui, c'est la nôtre;
   h) Ce sont les nôtres;
   i) ce sont les leurs;
   j) Ce sont les leurs;
   k) c'est la sienne;
   l) c'est la sienne.

Indefinite Pronouns (p. 62)

1. b) toutes; c) Toutes; d) tout;
   e) Tout; f) tous
2. a) Toutes ces cassettes sont à
   toi ? – Non, elles apparti-
   ennent toutes à ma sœur.
   b) Tu as lavé les pantalons ?
   – Oui, je les ai lavés tous.
   Chaque pantalon doit être
   lavé séparément.
   c) Pour la fête, je dois laver chaque assiette. Il faut
   qu'elles brillent toutes. Et
   chacune doit être rangée à sa
   place (bien) précise.
   d) Tous les enfants sont rentrés ? – Non, pas tous. Mais
   chaque enfant doit être à la
   maison à huit heures.
   e) Tu as tout mangé ? – Non,
   pas tout. Mais nous allons
   manger tous les restes demain.
   f) Il a dormi toute la journée.
   Il fait ça tous les jours.

Relative Pronouns (pp. 66 – 67)

1. b) que; c) qui, qui, qui; d) que;
   e) qui; f) que
2. b) La fille dont Jean a parlé est
   suisse.
   c) La ville dont nous avons vu
   un film s'appelle Marseille.
   d) Voilà Emma et Fanny dont la
   passion est la nourriture.
   e) J'ai vu une fille dont les
   parents habitent au Portugal.
3. b) dont / de qui; c) qui;
   d) auquel; e) dont; f) dont;
   g) à qui; h) que; i) que;
   j) où; k) laquelle; l) lesquelles;
   m) auxquels
4. b) Est-ce qu'il y a une ville que
   tu aimes mieux ?
   c) Non, San Francisco est la
   ville que j'aime le plus.
   d) Ma femme qui a 38 ans vient
   de New York City.
   e) New York City qui est plus
   célèbre que San Francisco est
   la ville qui plaît le plus à ma
   femme.
   f) Le fils de ma femme que tout
   le monde appelle Dodo est né
   à Chicago.
   g) La fille de mon amie qui a
   25 ans fait ses études à
   Dallas.

Present Tense (pp. 80 – 82)

1. b) épeler – tu épelles – nous
   épelons – elles épellent
   c) geler– je gèle – vous gelez –
   ils gèlent
   d) mener – elle mène – nous
   menons – ils mènent
   e) préférer – je préfère – vous
   préférez – elles préfèrent

f) placer – je place – tu places
– nous plaçons

g) nager – on nage – nous
nageons – ils nagent

h) envoyer – j'envoie – nous
envoyons – ils envoient

i) réussir – je réussis – vous
réussissez – elles réussissent

j) vendre – tu vends – nous
vendons – ils vendent

k) croire – tu crois – nous
croyons – ils croient

l) être – tu es – nous sommes –
ils sont

m) avoir – tu as – nous avons –
ils ont

2. b) sommes-nous, on est;

c) ils vont, ils traversent;

d) Asseyez-vous;

e) Bats-moi / Battez-moi;

f) est, boit; g) vous cuisez;

h) disparaît; i) il parcourt;

j) nous éteignons;

k) ils ne croient pas;

l) vous devez; m) nous dormons

n) s'écrit; o) il satisfait, ils veulent; p) élit; q) elle ne sent
plus; r) je ne permets pas;

s) elle souffre; t) se tait

3. b) Tous les jours, je reçois une
lettre de mon oncle.

c) Le magasin vend tous les
vêtements en solde.

d) Je me souviens de madame
Dutour.

e) Nous vivons une époque
difficile.

4. me traduis – ne veux pas –
ne me plaît pas – lis – vous
interdis – rejoint – n'ai pas soif
– meurs – veulent – ne crois pas
– pleut – ne veulent pas – fait –
descendons – allons – mangeons
– as – accepte – ne résous pas

5. b) Il a 25 ans.

c) Il fait ses études à Paris.

d) Il boit souvent du vin rouge.

e) Il habite seul. *oder:*
Il vit seul.

Compound Past (pp. 88 – 91)

1.

Infinitive with **avoir**	Compound Past	Infinitive with **être**	Compound Past
vendre	j'ai vendu	aller	je suis allé(e)
offrir	j'ai offert	venir	je suis venu(e)
être	j'ai été	se taire	je me suis tu(e)
courir	j'ai couru	tomber	je suis tombé(e)
pouvoir	j'ai pu	arriver	je suis arrivé(e)
pleuvoir	il a plu	se rendre	je me suis rendu(e)
rire	j'ai ri	s'offrir	je me suis offert
devoir	j'ai dû	rentrer	je suis rentré(e)
voyager	j'ai voyagé	se dire	je me suis dit

Answers

2. b) Il s'est assis.
   c) Il a pris le journal et il l'a lu.
   d) Il a commencé à faire son ménage.
   e) il est tombé par terre – il s'est mis debout.
   f) Il a marché un peu – il a descendu sa valise.
   g) Il a appelé un taxi – il est venu.
   h) Le monsieur est monté dans le taxi – la voiture a roulé.
   i) il a ouvert la porte.
   j) Puis le monsieur est descendu du taxi et est allé à l'hôpital.
   k) Un médecin est arrivé. Il a dit bonjour.
   l) Il l'a examiné.
   m) Puis le monsieur est parti. Mais devant l'hôpital, il est retombé.

3. b) il s'est acheté – il les a mangés
   c) il est allé – il a pris
   d) se sont promenés
   e) ils ont continué – il a conduit
   f) il a eu faim – il a lu
   g) ils sont entrés
   h) elle est venue – elle leur a montré
   i) ils ont pris
   j) elle est arrivée – elle la leur a donnée
   k) il a ouvert – rien ne lui a plu
   l) il a jeté
   n) ils ont descendu – ils ont quitté
   o) elle s'est tue – elle a ri
   p) ils sont montés – sont partis

Imperfect (pp. 95 – 96)

1. a) chantaient;
   b) luisait;
   c) pleuvait / avaient / recroque-villaient
   d) desséchait / était;
   e) tiraient
   f) se posait / revenait;
   g) pouvaient / faisait;
   h) entendait / jouaient;
   i) aimais / me plaignais;
   j) profitions / nous installions / se reposait

2. a) elle s'est levée;
   b) il faisait, on est allés;
   c) a bu, a commandé, a mangé, a payé;
   d) faisait des achats, il a vu;
   e) s'est promenée, elle a vu;
   f) avait, ils ont attendu;
   g) il préparait, a frappé;
   h) sont allés, ils ont pris;
   i) j'étais, je faisais, sont venus;
   j) elle se brossait, elle a oublié

Pluperfect (pp. 98 – 99)

1. b) il avait vécu;
   c) nous avions ri;
   d) elles avaient vu;
   e) tu avais mis; f) j'avais voulu;
   g) elle était allée;
   h) ils avaient pris;
   i) elles étaient venues;
   j) vous aviez su; k) j'avais fait;
   l) vous aviez dit;
   m) tu étais tombé(e);
   n) j'avais vaincu;
   o) ils avaient dormi;
   p) elle avait vécu; q) il était né;
   r) j'avais reçu; s) tu avais pu;
   t) ils étaient tombés;
   u) elle était arrivée;
   v) elles avaient été;
   w) j'avais eu; x) elle était restée

2. b) avait pris; c) avait reçu;
d) avait jeté

3. b) avons fait;
c) étions, ont raconté;
d) avaient passé;
e) avaient visité;
f) avaient impressionnés;
g) étaient allés;
h) avaient fait;
i) tournait, avaient peur;
j) étaient partis;
k) avaient assisté;
l) n'ont pas arrêté;
m) avons dit, sommes installés;
n) avons trouvé;
o) ont retrouvés, ont continué

Simple Past (p. 102)

1. b) a bu;
c) s'est mis, a fait;
d) a dit, ne lui a pas répondu;
e) s'est fâché, a eu;
f) ont lu;
g) se sont regardés, ont ri;
h) ont su; i) s'en sont allés,
se sont installés;
j) est venu, a vu;
k) a voulu

Future (pp. 108 – 110)

1. b) deviendrai; c) aurai;
d) aurons; e) travaillerai;
f) nous occuperons;
g) ferons construire;
h) joueront; i) verrai;
j) posséderai; k) irons;
l) pratiquerai, apprendrai;
m) pleuvra, lira; n) prendra;
o) enverrons

2. b) Tu vas dire bonjour à ta
mère.
c) A partir de demain, tu ne vas
plus boire.
d) A la montagne, nous allons
bien dormir.
e) Vous allez revenir l'année
prochaine ?
f) Demain soir, on va parler du
nouveau film.
g) Est-ce que nous allons faire
du ski pendant les vacances ?
h) J'espère qu'il ne va pas
pleuvoir demain.
i) Ma fille va être une grande
actrice.
j) Vous allez regarder un film
samedi prochain ?

3. b) Mais on n'ira plus à
Chamonix.
c) Mais on ne prendra plus de
chambre à l'hôtel.
d) Mais nous ne dormirons plus
dans une petite chambre.
e) Mais je ne m'ennuierai plus
sur la piste.
f) Mais je n'enverrai plus de
cartes postales à nos amis.
Je ne les tiendrai plus au
courant.
g) Mais il ne boira plus au bar.
Il ne s'installera plus au
comptoir.
h) Mais je ne serai plus fatiguée.
Je n'aurai plus sommeil.
i) Mais je ne verrai plus de
photo de mon mari dans un
journal.
j) Mais je ne ferai plus semblant
de ne rien voir.
k) Mais il ne me trompera plus.
l) Mais on ne verra plus mon
mari avec une autre femme.

Answers

Pages 112 – 127

Future Perfect (p. 112)

1. c) aura mis; d) aura passé;
   e) aura repassé; f) aura nettoyé;
   g) aura fait; h) sera allé;
   i) aura sorti; j) sera parti;
   k) se sera promené;
   l) sera rentré; m) se sera mis;
   n) serai revenue;
   o) sera préparés;
   p) sera allés; q) aura dansé;
   r) aura pris; s) sera rentrés;
   t) se sera couchés

Tip for p. 112, 1. i):

Sortir has a direct object here and therefore must be combined with **avoir**.

Conditional (pp. 116 / 117)

1. b) elles mettraient; c) on ferait;
   d) ils voudraient; e) tu devrais;
   f) il verrait; g) nous voudrions;
   h) elle dirait; i) j'irais;
   j) vous seriez; k) tu mangerais;
   l) ils suivraient; m) on vivrait;
   o) je tiendrais
2. b) Le président aurait menti.
   c) Le premier ministre aurait démissionné.
   d) Des rebelles auraient pris le pouvoir.
   e) Le parlement aurait été en flammes.
3. b) voudrais, aimerais;
   c) Auriez-vous;
   d) pourrais, raterais
4. b) Je voudrais / voulais vous demander si vous pourriez me prêter de l'argent.
   c) Nous pourrions aller au cinéma ce soir.
   d) Demande-lui s'il serait d'accord.
   e) Il m'a demandé si quelqu'un viendrait.
   f) Des troupes étrangères auraient assassiné le président.

g) Au cas où / Dans le cas où / Pour le cas où ils viendraient, tu prépares un petit déjeuner.
h) J'aurais dû apprendre un autre métier.
i) L'ambassadeur allemand serait mort.
j) Je pourrais manger une énorme glace maintenant.

Subjunctive (pp. 125 – 127)

1. b) qu'il dorme; c) qu'elle puisse;
   d) qu'il pleuve; e) que j'aille;
   f) que nous soyons;
   g) que vous finissiez;
   h) que tu prennes;
   i) qu'ils sachent; j) que j'écrive;
   k) qu'elles veuillent; l) que j'aie;
   m) que nous buvions;
   n) que vous preniez
2. b) Je souhaite qu'elle ne soit pas partie.
   c) J'exige qu'il travaille.
   d) J'aimerais qu'il soit sage.
   e) Je n'aime pas qu'elle lise au lit.
   f) Je demande que la phrase soit correcte.
   g) C'est surprenant qu'il ne pleure plus.
   h) Il est indispensable qu'elle sache compter.
   i) Il est normal qu'il veuille un téléviseur.
   j) Il est nécessaire qu'elle aille en vacances.
   k) Je trouve bien que tu n'achètes plus de viande.
   l) Je suis fâché qu'elle ne me tienne plus au courant.
   m) Je suis surprise qu'il ne boive plus.
   n) Je ne crois pas que tu sois contente.

222

3. a) allez, verb of probability: present or future
   b) avez fait; no subjunctive is used in indirect discourse
   c) apprennes; impersonal expression
   d) ait; impersonal expression
   e) est parti; after affirmative expressions of thinking and giving an opinion, no subjunctive is used
   f) passiez; verb expressing emotion
   g) fait; fact
   h) ayons passé; superlative with subjunctive assessment
   i) aille; impersonal expression
   j) réussisses; verb expressing desirability or insistence (volition)
4. 1d, 2e, 3i, 4a, 5g, 6h, 7f, 8b, 9c

Imperative (p. 130)

1. b) Donne-moi encore une réponse.
   c) Passe-moi l'éponge.
   d) Ferme-la fenêtre.
   e) Lisez un texte.
   f) Répondez-moi.
   g) Sortez vos livres.
   h) Sors ton livre.
   i) Commence à lire.
   j) Donnez-moi la réponse tout de suite.
   k) Soyez de bons élèves.
2. b) Ne vous asseyez pas.
   c) Ne te lève pas.
   d) Ne commence pas à le lire.
   e) Ne le nettoie pas.
   f) N'y va pas.
   g) Ne la complète pas.
   h) Ne me la dis pas.
   i) Ne me les donnez pas.
   j) N'y pensons pas.

Si Clause (pp. 133 – 134)

1. b) Si seulement l'appartement était plus grand.
   c) Si seulement je gagnais au loto.
   d) Si seulement j'avais un ami.
   e) Si seulement je travaillais moins.
   f) Si seulement j'allais en vacances cette année.
   g) Si seulement quelqu'un me rendait visite.
   h) Si seulement je vivais à Paris.
2. b) avait passé; c) venait;
   d) aimes; e) fait; f) ferais;
   g) aurais acheté; h) avais su
3. b) Si je gagne au loto, je m'achèterai une maison.
   c) Si je gagnais au loto, je m'achèterais une maison.
   d) Si mon ami était plus jeune, je me marierais avec lui.
   e) Si j'avais été riche, j'aurais acheté une maison.

Passive (p. 143)

1. b) Le pays a été occupé par la France au 17e siècle.
   c) Au 18e siècle, des forteresses ont été construites par Vauban.
   d) En 1871, la province d'Alsace a été annexée par l'Empire d'Allemagne.
   e) En 1945, l'Alsace a été libérée des Allemands par les alliés.
   f) Et prochainement, une nouvelle ligne de TGV sera ouverte par la SNCF.

Negation (pp. 148–150)

1. b) je ne veux pas de pomme.
   c) je ne veux pas de glace.
   d) je ne veux pas de nouveau T-shirt.
   e) Non, je ne veux pas faire de voyage en Espagne.
   f) Non, je ne veux pas de nouvelle amie.
2. b) Non, je n'ai pas mangé de sandwich.
   c) Non, je ne veux rien boire.
   d) Non, je n'ai pas encore parlé à mon professeur.
   e) Non, je ne vais inviter personne.
   f) Non, je n'ai rien vu.
   g) Non, je ne mange pas de viande (du tout).
   h) Non, ce n'est pas mon ami.
   i) Non, je n'adore pas la musique.
   j) Non, rien ne me manque.
   k) Non, je ne ferai plus de voyage.
   l) Non, je n'ai vu ni Barbara ni Michel.
   m) Non, ce n'est pas du fromage.
   n) Non, il n'a plus rien dit.
   o) Non, il n'a toujours pas trouvé de femme. / Non, il n'a pas encore trouvé de femme.
   p) Non, elle n'a toujours pas parlé à ses parents.
   q) Non, elle n'a plus parlé à personne.
   r) Non, nous ne regardons pas toujours la télé.
   s) Non, je n'ai pas encore passé mon permis de conduire.
   t) Non, je ne viendrai pas non plus.

3. a) Non, je ne lui ai pas encore écrit.
   b) Non, je n'y vais pas.
   c) Non, je n'ai rien acheté.
   d) Non, pas celui-ci.
   e) Non, je n'ai vu personne.
   f) Non, elle n'a plus rien dit.
   g) Non, je n'en mange plus.
   h) Non, elle n'a pas du tout changé.

Indirect Discourse (pp. 154 – 156)

1. b) qu' ... aimera;
   c) si ... n'en ai pas;
   d) que ... n'en ai pas vu;
   e) s' ... a fait;
   f) qu' ... ne me quittera jamais
2. b) Elle dit qu'elle veut que je fasse mes devoirs.
   c) Elle dit que je ne sortirai pas demain.
   d) Elle dit qu'elle se sent mieux si je reste à la maison.
   e) Elle demande si j'ai déjà rendu visite à mes grands-parents.
   f) Elle demande ce que je vais offrir à mon père pour son anniversaire.
   g) Elle demande si je pourrais l'aider à faire la vaisselle.
3. b) avais; c) était mariée;
   d) avait fait; e) quitterait;
   f) aimerait; g) pensais

4. b) Il veut savoir si elle l'appellera de Paris.

c) Il veut savoir s'il peut lui téléphoner de temps en temps.

d) Il veut savoir si elle lui apportera un petit cadeau.

e) Il veut savoir si sa sœur va l'accompagner.

f) Il veut savoir si elle ne va pas s'ennuyer sans lui.

g) Il veut savoir ce qu'il va faire sans elle.

5. b) Il m'a demandé quand je les avais faits.

c) Il voulait savoir si quelqu'un m'avait aidé à les faire.

d) Il m'a demandé si je pouvais lui répondre correctement.

e) Il a dit qu'il ne croyait pas que je puisse lui donner une traduction correcte.

f) Il a ajouté que pour cette traduction j'allais avoir une mauvaise note.

g) Il a dit qu'il appellerait mes parents le jour même.

h) Il a ajouté que je devrais lui rendre cette lettre le lendemain.

i) Il a précisé que la prochaine fois, j'irais voir le directeur.

j) Il m'a demandé ce que je faisais pendant tout l'après-midi.

k) Il voulait savoir si j'avais déjà pensé à mon avenir.

l) Il a dit qu'il y avait trente ans, un élève comme moi n'aurait pas travaillé comme ça.

Adjectives (pp. 170 – 173)

1. b) rare; c) secret; d) européenne; e) fausse; f) aiguë; g) publique; h) facile; i) réel; j) frais; k) turque; l) grecque; m) vif; n) amère; o) nette; p) grosse; q) blanche; r) jaloux; s) suisse; t) russe; u) bon marché; v) citron; w) complète; x) grasse

2. a) mauvais – mauvais – mauvaise – mauvaises

b) fatal – fatals – fatale – fatales

c) gris – gris – grise – grises

d) long – longs – longue – longues

e) amical – amicaux – amicale – amicales

f) beau / bel – beaux – belle – belles

g) vieux / vieil – vieux – vieille – vieilles

h) dur – durs – dure – dures

i) gentil – gentils – gentille – gentilles

j) frais – frais – fraîche – fraîches

k) européen – européens – européenne – européennes

l) sec – secs – sèche – sèches

3. a) une nouvelle maison

b) une grande salle de séjour – une salle de bains minuscule – quatre petites chambres

c) un travail fatigant – cette vieille maison

d) ma pauvre mère

e) ce sale travail – dernier moment

f) de longs travaux – une maison propre

g) le seul défaut – sa mauvaise isolation

4. b) Il a des cheveux bruns.
   c) Elle fait une sauce légère.
   d) Ils font partie de l'église catholique.
   e) Tu écris avec la main gauche.
   f) Je lis un gros livre.
   g) Vous racontez une brève histoire.
   h) Elle arrive avec une jambe cassée.
   i) Ils préfèrent la nourriture turque.
   j) Je vois une pièce franco-allemande.
   k) Elle contacte un certain Yves.
   l) Elles portent des robes longues.
   m) Il s'achète une voiture nouvelle.
   n) Elle mène une vie simple.
   o) Ils ont passé l'examen la semaine dernière.
   p) Il est mon seul ami.
   q) Mes parents ont un grand appartement.

5. b) Monique est plus grande que Florence.
   c) La voiture de M. Dutour est plus neuve que celle / la voiture de M. Floret.
   d) Une chambre à l'Hôtel de Provence est plus chère qu'à l'Hôtel de Normandie.
   e) Olivier est meilleur que Marc.
   f) Michel est pire que Barbara.

Adverbs (pp. 181 – 182)

1. b) absolument – gentiment – généreusement – extrêmement
   c) bien – vite / conduire / rouler vite
   d) franchement – lentement
   e) dur – français – terriblement – mal – profondément – précisément – mieux

2. b) énormément;
   c) profondément;
   d) suffisamment; e) bien;
   f) gentiment; g) vraiment;
   h) poliment; i) complètement;
   j) rarement; k) brièvement;
   l) lentement; m) absolument;
   n) extrêmement;
   o) courageusement;
   p) conformément;
   q) précisément

3. a) heureusement;
   b) récemment, récente;
   c) énorme, énormément;
   d) complète, complètement;
   e) mieux, meilleure;
   f) mal, mauvaise; g) bien, bien;
   h) bon, bien

Numbers and Telling Time (pp. 189 – 190)

1. b) 1er septembre 1939;
   c) 11 novembre 1918;
   d) 1er janvier 2000

2. b) quinze heures dix-huit
   c) vingt heures quinze
   d) zéro heure vingt
   e) huit heures trente
   f) douze heures quarante-cinq
   g) seize heures
   h) deux heures cinquante

3. b) cinq heures et demie
c) sept heures moins le quart
d) dix heures vingt
e) midi
f) minuit
g) six heures moins dix
h) huit heures moins cinq
i) cinq heures et demie
j) six heures et demie
k) trois heures et quart
l) six heures moins le quart
m) deux heures cinq
n) huit heures (pile)
o) trois heures et demie

4. b) vingt et un;
c) un demi, un quart;
d) un huitième;
e) une quinzaine;
f) un exercice sur cinq;
g) deux cents, deux cent cinquante;
h) cinquante mille;
i) quatre-vingts, quatre-vingt-deux;
j) huit mille cinq cent soixante

Prepositions (pp. 198 – 200)

1. à Paris – au Portugal – au / dans le sud de la France – à Grenoble – dans le Bas-Rhin – en Italie – à Cuba – aux Pays-Bas – à pied – au cinéma – en voiture – en Suisse – à la montagne – au Japon – en Bourgogne – dans le Var – en train – à moto

2. a) de la gare; b) au sud de Paris; c) chez le médecin; d) de Brest; e) à la campagne; f) dans les Alpes; g) à Washington aux Etats-Unis

3. B. : au
M. : le – au – le
B. : en – en – au – en – A – l' – le – en – au – le
B. : au – le – au – le – en – à – le – Au – en – au – en – le – Dans les – en – en – à

4. b) En juin et juillet / Aux mois de juin et juillet
c) à deux heures du matin
d) à trois heures / pour trois heures / en trois heures / vers trois heures
e) dans quinze jours
f) pour six mois / il y a six mois / depuis six mois
g) il y a trois mois
h) jusqu'à deux heures / pendant deux heures / à partir de deux heures

5. a) à Annick mais à Pascal;
b) Dans quinze jours, en avion;
c) par avion; d) à café, à thé;
e) de café; f) en cristal / de cristal, pour 200 euros
g) A midi, dans la rue;
h) de A à Z

Conjunctions (pp. 204 – 205)

1. b) choisisses; c) aura payé;
d) aura quitté; e) vienne;
f) habite; g) faisait;
h) ai voulu – a répondu

2. b) serait fermée; c) ait;
d) serait; e) vienne

3. b) Dès que tu seras arrivé, nous irons manger.
   c) Puisque tu es végétarien, nous ne mangerons pas de viande.
   d) Pendant que je t'écris, je regarde un film.
   e) J'ai économisé beaucoup d'argent pour que nous puissions aller dans un bon restaurant.

The Interrogative Sentence (pp. 213–214)

1. b) D'où; c) Quand; d) De qui;
   e) A quoi; f) A qui
2. b) Qui est-ce qui;
   c) Qu'est-ce qu';
   d) Qui est-ce qu';
   e) Qu'est-ce qui;
   f) Qu'est-ce que;
   g) Qui est-ce qui;
   h) Qu'est-ce qui

3. b) Va-t-il en France pour faire des études ?
   c) Avez-vous voyagé beaucoup ?
   d) Prenez-vous souvent l'avion ?
   e) N'a-t-elle pas pris la voiture ?
   f) Votre femme connaît-elle déjà la nouvelle collection ?
   g) Votre mari va-t-il en ville demain ?
   h) Le président n'a-t-il pas donné une interview ?
4. b) Lesquelles ?; c) Duquel ?;
   d) Chez lequel ?; e) Lesquelles ?;
   f) Desquels ?; g) Auquel ?;
   h) A laquelle ?; i) De laquelle ?

Overview of Grammatical Terms

English	French
active	actif
adjective	adjective
adverb	adverbe
adverbial modifier	complément circonstanciel
adverbial pronoun	pronom adverbial
article	article
cardinal number	nombre cardinal
collective number	nombre collectif
comparative (degree)	comparatif
compound past	passé composé
conditional	conditionnel
conditional clause, si clause	proposition conditionnelle
conjugate	conjuguer
conjunction	conjunction
consonant	consonne
dative	datif
dative object	complément d'objet indirect
demonstrative determiner	adjectif démonstratif
demonstrative pronoun	pronom démonstratif
direct object	complément d'objet direct
feminine	féminin
fraction	nombre fractionnaire
future	futur
gender	genre
imperative	impératif
imperfect	imparfait
indefinite determiner	adjectif indéfini
indefinite pronoun	pronom indéfini
indicative	indicatif
indirect discourse	discours indirect
indirect object	complément d'objet indirect
infinitive	infinitif
interrogative determiner	adjectif interrogatif

Grammatical Terms

English	French
interrogative pronoun	pronom interrogatif
masculine	masculin
mood, mode	mode
negation	négation
nominative	nominatif
noun	nom
noun determiner	déterminant du nom
number	nombre
object	complément d'objet
object pronoun	pronom personnel complément
ordinal number	ordinal
past participle	participe passé
passive	passif
personal pronoun	pronom personnel
pluperfect	plus-que-parfait
plural	pluriel
possessive determiner	adjectif possessif
possessive pronoun	pronom possessif
preposition	préposition
present (tense)	présent
pronoun	pronom
reflexive pronoun	pronom réfléchi
reflexive verb	verbe pronominal
relative pronoun	pronom relatif
singular	singulier
subject	sujet
subject pronoun	pronom personnel sujet
subjunctive	subjonctif
superlative (degree)	superlatif
tense	temps
verb	verbe
vowel	voyelle

Index

A

à 22, 47–50, 191–196
à condition que 123, 201–202
à moins que 123, 201–202
à object 47–48, 135–136, 206, 210–211
à supposer que 123, 201–202
adjectives 157–169
adverbial pronouns 47–50
adverbs 174–180
affix 9, 12
afin que 123, 201–202
after the time of speaking 68–69
aller 74, 104–106, 120
après 195
après que 201
articles 21–25
au cas où 114, 201–203
au, aux 22
aucun 144–145
au-dessous de 193
au-dessus de 193
aussi ... que 168, 177
autant 178
autour de 193
avant 195
avant que 201–202
avec 196
avoir 74, 84, 100, 105, 118, 129
avoir or *être* ? 84–85

B

beau, bel, belle 160–161, 165
beaucoup 179
before the time of speaking 68–69
bien 176, 179–180
bien que 201–202
bon 159, 165, 169, 176, 178

C

c'est, ce sont 53, 56, 206, 210
ça 56
cardinal numbers 183–184
ce 28–29, 56, 61
ce qui, ce que 65, 152
cela 56
celui, celle 55
certain(s) 36, 61, 166
ceux 55, 61
chacun 60–61
chaque 36
chez 193
-ci 29, 55
collective numbers 186
color adjectives 163
comme 201, 203
comparative (degree) 168
comparisons 168–169, 177–178
compound past *(passé composé)* 83–87, 93–94
compound past or imperfect? 93–94
conjunctions 201–203
contre 193

D

dans 192, 195
days of the week 23, 188
de 22, 47–48, 162, 193, 196
de façon que 201–203
de manière que 201, 203
de object 136, 211
de sorte que 201, 203
declarative sentence 49–50, 206–207
definite article 21–23, 188
demi 163, 186
demonstrative determiners 28–29
demonstrative pronouns 55–56

département names 23
depuis 195
depuis que 201–202
derrière 193
dès 195
dès que 201
determiners 21–39
devant 193
direct object 42, 60, 64–65, 86, 135–136, 141, 164, 206
direct object pronoun 41–43, 50, 135–136
direction of movement 85
dont 64
du tout 147
du, de la, des 22, 24

E

en 47–50, 128, 135, 192, 195–196
entre 64, 193, 195
est-ce que question 208
étant donné que 201, 203
être 74, 84, 92, 100, 105, 118, 129
eux 50, 53

F

faire 76, 84, 100, 105, 120
falloir 76, 84, 105, 120, 139
finir 74, 104
formation of adjective plurals 161–162
formation of noun plurals 17–18
fractions 186
future perfect 111

G

gender (of nouns) 15–17
giving the date 23, 188
grand 163, 166

Index

I

il   41–44, 139–140
il y a   139, 195
imperative   50, 128–129
imperfect   92–94
impersonal verbs and
    expressions   122, 139–140
indefinite article   24–25
indefinite determiners   35–36
indefinite pronouns   60–61
indirect discourse   151–153
indirect object   43, 47–48, 86
indirect object pronouns   41–
    44, 48, 50, 135
interrogative
    determiners   38–39
interrogative pronouns   209–
    211
interrogative sentence   49–
    50, 208–212
intonation question   208
inversion question   208–209
irregular verbs   75–79

J

jamais   144–145
jusqu'à ce que   123, 201–202
jusque   188, 193, 195

L

-là   29, 55
la plupart   25
le mien   58
le moins   169, 177
le plus   169, 177–178
le, la, les   21–23, 41–44, 49,
    135
lequel   63–64, 212
leur   41–44, 49, 86, 135
leur, leurs   31–33, 58
loin de   194
lorsque   201
lui   41–44, 49–50, 53, 86,
    135

M

mal   176, 178
mauvais   165, 169, 176, 178
me   41–44, 49–50
meilleur   165, 169, 176
-ment   174–175
mieux   176–178
modal prepositions   196
moi   50, 53, 129
moindre   165, 169
moins … que   168, 177–178
mon, ma, mes   31–33
mood (mode)   70

N

names of countries   23
names of islands   23
names of provinces   23
ne … pas / que   144–147
ne … que   147
near future   106–107
negation   25, 49, 144–147
ni   147
non   144
non plus   147
noun   15–18
nouveau, nouvel,
    nouvelle   160, 163, 166
numbers   48, 183–187

O

object   42–44
object pronouns   41–44, 49,
    60, 63
on   42, 49, 85, 142
ordinal numbers   185
où   65, 152, 211
oui   144

P

par   194, 196
paraître   139
parce que   201, 203
parmi   64, 194
(ne…) pas   144–145
pas de   145

passive   141–142
past conditional   115
past participle   83–86
past subjunctive   121–124
pendant   195
pendant que   201
personal pronouns   41–44, 53
personne   144–146
petit   165, 169
peu   177
pire   169
placement of adjectives   165–
    167
placement of adverbs   176
placement of negation   144–
    145
placement of object and
    adverbial pronouns   49–50
pluperfect *(plus-que-*
    parfait)   97
(ne…) plus   144–146
plus … que   168, 177–178
plusieurs   36, 61
possessive determiners   31–
    33, 58
possessive pronouns   58
pour   194–195, 197
pour que   201–202
pourvu que   123, 201–202
pouvoir   77, 84, 100, 105, 120
prefix   9, 12
prepositions   191–197
près de   194
present (tense)   71–79
present conditional   113–114
present subjunctive   118–
    120, 122–124
probe question   209, 212
pronouns   41–65
proper names   18
puisque   201, 203

Q

qu'est-ce qui / que   209–211
quand   132, 152, 212
que   53, 64, 151–152

que clause   121–124
quel   38–39, 152, 210
qui   63–65, 152, 210–211
qui est-ce qui / que   209–211
quoi   152, 211
quoique   123, 201–202

R
reflexive pronouns   44, 86
reflexive verbs   44, 85–86,
   137–138, 142
relative clause   55, 61, 124
relative pronouns   63–65
replacement of the
   passive   141–142
rien   144–145

S
sans que   123, 201–202
savoir   78, 84, 100, 105, 120,
   129
se   44, 137–138, 142
se faire + infinitive   142
sembler   140, 164
seulement   147
si   131–132, 144
si clause   131–132
silent h   21, 29, 32, 43
simple future   103–105, 107

simple past *(passé
   simple)*   100–101
sous   194
statements of place   23, 47,
   191, 207
statements of quantity   25,
   48
statements of time   35, 153,
   187, 207
stem   73, 92
stem vowel   119
stressed (disjunctive) personal
   pronouns   48, 50, 53
stressed on ending   120
subject pronouns   41–42
suffix   9–14
superlative (degree)   169
sur   194, 197

T
tandis que   201
tant que   201
telling time   187
tense   68–69
times of day   23
tout   35–36, 60–61, 180
très   179
trop   175, 179
type of movement   84

U
unstressed personal
   pronouns   41–44

V
variability of the past
   participle   85–86
verb stem   9, 73
verbs expressing a direction of
   movement   85
verbs expressing a type of
   movement   84
verbs of the 1st group   73–74
verbs of the 2nd group   74
verbs of the 3rd group   74–79
verbs with an object   135–
   136
vieux, vieil, vieille   160, 165
vouloir   79, 84, 101, 105, 120
vu que   201, 203

W
word formation   9–14

Y
y   47–50, 128, 135
year dates   184

Notes

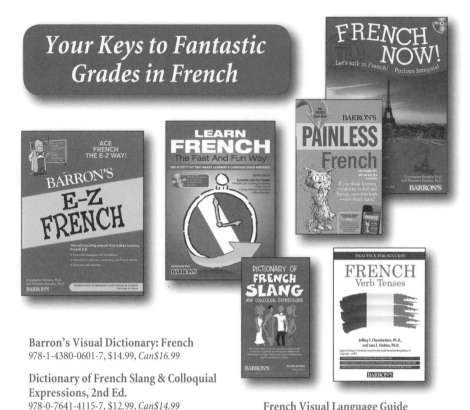